SPOOKED!

How a Radio Broadcast and *The War of the Worlds*
Sparked the 1938 Invasion of America

GAIL JARROW

CALKINS CREEK
AN IMPRINT OF HIGHLIGHTS
Honesdale, Pennsylvania

Excerpts from the script of *The War of the Worlds* radio broadcast reprinted by permission of ICM Partners. Copyright © 1940 by Hadley Cantril (In *Invasion from Mars*), © renewed 1967 by Howard Koch.

Calkins Creek
An Imprint of Highlights
815 Church Street
Honesdale, Pennsylvania 18431
calkinscreekbooks.com
Printed in China

ISBN: 978-1-62979-776-2 (hc)
ISBN: 978-1-68437-143-3 (eBook)
Library of Congress Control Number: 2018933314

First edition

10 9 8 7 6 5 4 3 2 1

Designed by Red Herring Design

Contents

CHAPTER ONE
8 HAUNTED ON HALLOWEEN EVE

CHAPTER TWO
14 MERCURY RISES

CHAPTER THREE
21 TAKING TO THE AIR

CHAPTER FOUR
25 BLOOD-RED PLANET

CHAPTER FIVE
29 PLOTTING THE INVASION

CHAPTER SIX
34 THE FINAL DAY

CHAPTER SEVEN
40 THE ATTACK

CHAPTER EIGHT
52 PANIC

CHAPTER NINE
56 "WRECKAGE"

CHAPTER TEN
67 IT'S ALL OVER

CHAPTER ELEVEN
74 EXTRA! EXTRA!
READ ALL ABOUT IT!

80 DEAR MR. WELLES

CHAPTER TWELVE
83 FALLOUT

91 DEAR FCC

CHAPTER THIRTEEN
94 "TOO DARN REALISTIC"

CHAPTER FOURTEEN
98 SOFT LANDING

104 HOAXES
108 TIMELINE
110 MORE TO EXPLORE
118 AUTHOR'S NOTE
120 SOURCE NOTES
131 SELECTED BIBLIOGRAPHY
135 INDEX
139 PICTURE CREDITS

For Oona Joan—
may you never be Spooked!

Acknowledgments

THANK YOU to these people who shared their time and expertise with me as I worked on this book.

For providing background on human psychology and behavior and for answering my questions about individual responses to media: J. Edward Russo, professor of Marketing, S. C. Johnson Graduate School of Management, Cornell University; and Michael Shapiro, professor, Department of Communication, Cornell University.

For filling me in on key aspects of radio broadcasting and sound production: Tish Pearlman, broadcast journalist and producer; and Nate Richardson, producer and musician.

For providing assistance with primary source research: the staffs at the Special Collections Library, University of Michigan, Ann Arbor; and at the National Archives, College Park, Maryland.

For help in locating and obtaining difficult-to-find photographs: Jeremy Megraw and Thomas Lisanti of the New York Public Library.

For their considerable skill in transforming a manuscript into a published book: the Calkins Creek team.

And for her dependable counsel on all my historical adventures: my trusty editor, Carolyn P. Yoder.

—GJ

A family gathers around the radio set. In the 1930s, listening
to the radio was Americans' favorite entertainment. By 1938,
about 80 percent of American homes had a radio.

CHAPTER ONE

HAUNTED ON HALLOWEEN EVE

"We figured our friends and families were all dead." —*New Jersey college student*

Mischief Night 1938 was crisp and clear in the northeastern United States. Following the tradition of the region, teens and older children prowled their neighborhoods. They soaped windows, smashed carved pumpkins, and toilet-papered bushes. The mischief-makers planned to return to the scene of their tricks the next night, Halloween, dressed in costume, innocently asking the neighbors for treats.

Few Americans knew that a group of adults was plotting a different sort of mischief for October 30, 1938.

That Sunday evening began with people gathered around the family radio, relaxing as the weekend drew to a close. On Monday morning, the young would be back at school. Men and some of the women would report to their jobs, if they were lucky enough to have one.

Radio was an escape from the challenges and concerns of their lives. The music, sports, comedy, and drama programs helped them forget the money troubles they'd had since the Great Depression began nine years earlier. Millions were still unemployed, doubtful about ever finding work again. Those with jobs weren't sure how long they would keep them. Many had lost their houses and farms because they couldn't pay their debts.

Lately, it seemed as if the bad news wouldn't stop. In September, a powerful hurricane pounded the East Coast from New York through New England. The storm hit without warning, killing about seven hundred people, damaging thousands of homes, and toppling millions of trees.

The ominous developments overseas added to the public's worries. Europe was on edge again just twenty years after the Great War tore it apart. Nations watched warily as Germany's power grew again. The country's dictator, Adolf Hitler, had broken international treaties and built up his military force. In March 1938, he took control of Austria and, in early October, part of what was then known as Czechoslovakia. Anxious Americans feared what the war-mongering Hitler might do next.

As the Sunday program was about to begin, men leaned back in a favorite chair. Women settled nearby, stitching the final touches onto Halloween costumes. Children who had finished their homework and returned from Mischief Night pranks lay on the floor by the radio set. Someone in the family switched it on and twirled the dial to the evening's entertainment.

During the Great Depression, which began in late 1929, businesses across the United States closed down, putting millions of people out of work. Police in New York City distribute bread and eggs to the unemployed in 1930.

The aftermath of the Hurricane of 1938 in Amherst, Massachusetts. On September 21, the storm devastated the East Coast from New York through New England.

About three minutes into the broadcast, an announcer's deep voice suddenly broke in with a special news bulletin. There had been reports of strange, unexplained explosions. The announcer promised that when more details were available, he would pass them on.

The regular program resumed.

Not long after, a commentator informed the audience that he had just been handed a telegram. It said that a "shock of almost earthquake intensity" had occurred close to Princeton, New Jersey. So far, the cause was unknown.

During the next fifteen minutes, radio listeners throughout the country heard the frightening updates. An invading army had attacked New Jersey. Eyewitnesses described the killings of dozens of people—state troopers, innocent bystanders, anyone who stood in the invaders' way. The commentator at the scene was hit by a powerful weapon, his entire body charred. New Jersey's state militia was deployed to confront the enemy with seven thousand heavily armed infantry soldiers.

Later, an announcer grimly told the audience that the militia had been overwhelmed in battle. Only 120 of the soldiers survived.

According to accounts, enemy fighters now controlled the middle section of New Jersey. They had cut off communications, pulled down power lines, demolished bridges, and ripped up railroad tracks. Cars full of terrified people streamed onto the highways, trying to escape. Officials declared martial law in New Jersey and parts of Pennsylvania.

At half past the hour, a familiar voice came over the airwaves. Was that President Franklin Roosevelt urging the nation to stay calm? Listeners wondered how they

Adolf Hitler (1889–1945) salutes his fellow Nazis at a rally in Germany in 1935. After building up his country's military, Hitler set into motion his plan to take over Europe.

could possibly remain calm when lethal black smoke was drifting over the landscape and the enemy was moving toward New York City. Millions of New Yorkers had fled by car or boat. Thousands had jumped into the river, frantically swimming from the danger.

Soon, news bulletins announced that military defenses had been destroyed. The invaders had swept west to Buffalo, Chicago, and St. Louis. Confirming the radio listeners' worst fears, a downcast voice lamented, "They wrecked the greatest country in the world."

No one foresaw the 1938 invasion. Not the military. Not political leaders. Not law enforcement officials. Not journalists. All were stunned by the events that Sunday night in October. And by the next morning, lives had been changed forever.

CHAPTER TWO

MERCURY RISES

" From the day young Orson landed at my school, … he was searching for some bizarre way to disturb people."

—*Headmaster, the Todd School for Boys*

Several years before the night of the invasion, two ambitious men met during the depths of the Great Depression.

They had different backgrounds, skills, and temperaments. One was organized, composed, and practical. The other was wildly creative, intense, and arrogant. Yet together they forced millions of people to sit up and take notice.

THE PRODUCER

The older of the two was born in Bucharest, Romania, on September 22, 1902. His French businessman father and British mother named him Jacques Haussmann. Though this would remain the son's legal name until he was forty years old, Jacques began using an English version, John Houseman, when he was in his early twenties.

Because of his family history and European childhood, Houseman learned four languages by the time he was five years old—French, English, German, and Romanian. His parents sent him to school in England, where he excelled academically and developed an interest in theatre and writing.

After winning a prestigious scholarship, Houseman seemed destined to attend a British university. But his father died, leaving his mother with limited income. Passing up the scholarship, the seventeen-year-old went to work to support her.

His late father's friends helped Houseman get jobs in companies that bought and sold grain throughout the world. Over the next decade, he built a successful career and started his own company based in New York City.

In his spare time, Houseman enjoyed going to the theatre and hanging out with

John Houseman
(1902–1988) used
his experience
as businessman,
writer, and director
to succeed as a
theatre producer.

friends who worked as actors, writers, and artists. He wrote magazine essays and articles and a book of short stories.

Then, in October 1929, the stock market crashed. The economy worldwide fell into depression, and like many others, Houseman's company went bankrupt.

His business in shambles, he decided he had nothing to lose by following his dream of a full-time writing career. The early 1930s were difficult years to make a living in any profession, let alone the arts. But Houseman's talent helped him find work writing theatre scripts and directing plays. More importantly, he later said, he earned "a reputation ... for organizing ability, taste and a capacity for creative collaboration."

George Orson Welles (1915–1985), age ten, pictured in a Wisconsin newspaper article about his precocious accomplishments

Drawing on his business, writing, and directing experience, Houseman became a skillful theatre producer. He had a knack for pulling together a group of artistic people, guiding them in staging a play, raising money, and managing the finances.

In his role as a producer, Houseman met his partner in the October 1938 plot.

MAN OF DECEPTION

At ten o'clock one winter evening in early 1935, Houseman slipped backstage at a New York production of Shakespeare's *Romeo and Juliet*. After tipping the doorman to get access to the dressing rooms, he climbed the stairs to the third floor. The play was still in progress, and Houseman heard the actors' voices on the stage below. He knew that the man he had come to see had been killed off. At least, his character had.

Houseman found the young actor sitting in his dressing room, his costume and fake beard lying to the side. Even without the beard, Orson Welles had so expertly concealed his facial features under heavy makeup and a false nose that he was unrecognizable.

Getting right to the point, Houseman explained the show he was producing. The main character was an aging banker who jumps to his death after being financially ruined. Houseman handed Welles the script. "Would you like to play this thing?" he asked.

The actor agreed to look it over. As they went their separate ways that night, Houseman hoped the challenge of the role would appeal to Welles.

Welles appeared two days later in Houseman's office, eager to formally audition for the part in front of the playwright, Archibald MacLeish. When Houseman heard Welles read, he knew that his hunch about the actor had been right.

The play was demanding because the dialogue was in blank verse. Welles delivered the lines flawlessly in his deep, reverberating voice, described by a critic as "[taking] possession of a theatre." A master of deception, the young actor brought to life the role of a man in his late fifties—impressive because he was just nineteen.

ACTING OUT

George Orson Welles had been impressing people since he was a toddler. Born on May 6, 1915, in Kenosha, Wisconsin, he was doted on by his mother, an accomplished pianist and suffragette. Certain that he was a genius, she treated the little boy as if he were an adult. After the family moved to Chicago when Welles was three, she exposed him to the city's finest music, art, and theatre.

By age ten, Orson had already made headlines. While he was back living in Wisconsin and attending elementary school, a Madison newspaper ran an article about his precocious accomplishments. His photograph appeared under the headline "Cartoonist, Actor, Poet and only 10." The boy, the story reported, not only wrote, directed, and acted in his school's plays, but he also illustrated and edited his summer camp's newsletter. The article went on to list Orson's additional talents as an oil painter, magician, and makeup artist.

Welles later admitted, "Everybody told me from the moment I was able to hear that I was absolutely marvelous."

Yet Welles's childhood was one of upheaval. His parents permanently separated when he was four. His mother died five years later, leaving her son with his wealthy businessman father, an alcoholic and gambler.

When Welles was eleven, his father enrolled him in a private boarding school for boys near Chicago. The Todd School allowed young Orson to take control of the student stage productions. He directed the actors, the lighting, and the set design.

"The theatre was totally Orson's," a former classmate recalled. "It was a one-man band."

Several months before Orson graduated from high school, his father died. His new guardian—a longtime family friend—urged the fifteen-year-old to attend college the following fall. Orson had other ideas. He'd always been successful in getting adults to do what he wanted, and this time was no different. His guardian gave in and allowed a sketching and painting trip to Ireland instead.

Once Orson arrived there, he pursued his true passion—theatre. He lied about his age and landed a part with a Dublin theatre group. At only sixteen, he played a middle-aged duke.

By 1934, Welles had acted his way from Ireland to New York City, where he became a member of an American theatre company. One New York reviewer wrote of him: "Although he is physically graceless offstage, pudgy and unathletic, his size [six feet two inches] and booming voice give him an authoritative . . . stage presence."

Welles's exceptional voice also won him roles on radio dramas—work that paid much better than those in the theatre. Houseman later said of Welles's vocal talents: "He was capable of expressing an almost unlimited range of moods and emotions."

Radio broadcasting was still new, but it had rapidly expanded in the past dozen years. The programs on the national networks were broadcast live. Because actors were not usually identified by name, the best ones performed in various roles without the audience knowing it.

Some weeks, Welles voiced characters on two dozen programs. He was so busy that he often read his scripted lines for the first time the moment he stepped in front of the microphone for the broadcast. His most famous role was "The Shadow," a crime fighter who defeated enemies using extraordinary powers, including invisibility.

To people in New York's entertainment world, Orson Welles seemed older and more sophisticated than the other young midwesterners who came to New York City to find fame. Welles played this role to perfection.

THE PARTNERSHIP

After working together on the play in 1935, Houseman and Welles realized the advantages of combining their talents. By spring of 1936, they were staging plays in New York City for the Federal Theatre Project (FTP).

The FTP was established in 1935 under the Works Progress Administration, one of the government's New Deal programs intended to provide economic relief during the Great Depression. The FTP employed nearly fifteen thousand writers, actors, directors, designers, and stage technicians. Theatre groups in towns and cities across the United States presented live dramas, comedies, and musicals at prices affordable to struggling families.

With Houseman as producer, Welles directed and acted. Audiences applauded their unconventional and inventive productions. Theatre critics approved. This praise didn't help when the two men went too far by putting on a play, *The Cradle Will Rock*, about labor strikes and corporate corruption. Their government bosses considered it too political, and in the summer of 1937, Houseman and Welles were fired.

Within two months, the partners raised enough money to form their own Broadway theatre company. They named it the Mercury Theatre, inspired by a copy of *The American Mercury* magazine lying around Welles's rented summer house. Using a stable troupe of actors, the Mercury Theatre presented a series of plays. The reviews were generally positive, and a theatre critic called one production "an exciting excursion into stagecraft."

Houseman admired the "innate dramatic instinct" Welles brought to each show. But the young man's enormous ego often caused problems that Houseman had to smooth over. Welles insisted on controlling set design, costumes, and props, as well as directing and acting. A perfectionist, he often lost his temper and patience. "Very few people argued with Orson about anything," one of the Mercury actors later remarked. "He was difficult."

WONDER BOY

The press, however, regarded Orson Welles as a wonder boy. In May 1938, *Time* magazine called him "the brightest moon that has risen over Broadway in years." The twenty-three-year-old appeared on the magazine's cover, disguised by the makeup and shaggy gray wig he wore for the role of an eighty-year-old character in one of the Mercury's plays.

The advertising poster for the 1936 play *Horse Eats Hat*, a production staged by Welles and Houseman for the Federal Theatre Project in New York City

Along with the flattering publicity came an offer from the CBS Radio Network. Would Welles be interested in having his own weekly radio program?

Scheduled to run that summer, the show would consist of one-hour dramas based on familiar novels and stories. CBS wanted to appeal to listeners who enjoyed programs more serious than the comedy and variety shows. The network hadn't found a sponsor, such as a cereal or soap company. That meant the budget would be modest.

Orson Welles, age twenty-one and already a star of theatre and radio

Despite these drawbacks, Welles jumped at the chance to reach millions of people with his own dramatic productions. His work as a voice actor taught him how influential radio was. About 80 percent of the country's thirty million homes had a radio, about double those with a telephone. The average listener tuned in five hours a day. In fact, listening to radio broadcasts ranked as Americans' favorite recreation—more popular than movies, books, or sports events.

By accepting the CBS deal, Welles became the program's host, star, director, and producer. His Mercury partner, John Houseman, performed his usual role behind the scenes managing business matters as co-producer. For the radio project, Houseman added writer and editor to his duties. The Mercury Theatre's regular actors rounded out the team.

They all knew how to weave a story onstage that transfixed an audience. Now they would cast their magic spell over the airwaves.

At nine o'clock Monday night, July 11, 1938, the Mercury Theatre broadcast its first radio drama. It was an adaptation of Bram Stoker's novel *Dracula*.

The October invasion was just four months away.

CHAPTER THREE

TAKING TO THE AIR

"Before we know what is happening, the story has come to life."

—*Newspaper review of* The Mercury Theatre on the Air

By late summer 1938, the Mercury team had settled into a rhythm. CBS proudly advertised Orson Welles's radio program as "the brightest sensation of the drama season."

Each week, Welles and Houseman chose a book to adapt for their broadcast. They picked the adventure stories *Treasure Island*, *A Tale of Two Cities*, and *The Count of Monte Cristo*, as well as the classics *Jane Eyre* and *Julius Caesar*. The men soon discovered how difficult it was to condense a novel into sixty pages, the average script length for a one-hour program.

WORDS, SOUNDS, MUSIC

Despite Houseman's skill in writing short stories and theatre scripts, he had no experience with radio. As the partners worked together on each adaptation, Welles taught him the techniques peculiar to radio. For the early shows, they hammered out the scripts together. By August, Houseman had taken on most of the writing himself.

He designed each story to hook the audience within minutes so that people didn't turn the dial to another program. Right away, the script had to reveal where the story was happening and who the characters were, providing enough details for the listener to form a mental picture. Yet the plot couldn't be cluttered with too many settings and characters because the audience kept track without visual hints.

The presentation mattered, too. The listener's imagination was fired by sound alone. From his years performing on radio dramas, Welles understood that the actors' voices and their words must be spellbinding.

Sound effects and music were just as important. For the first show, *Dracula*, Welles simulated the sound of a stake being driven through the vampire's heart by cracking

Welles (standing) and Houseman (left) in rehearsal for a 1936 theatre production

open a watermelon with a hammer. In *A Tale of Two Cities*, when the guillotine chops off a head, the sound effects team hacked a cabbage with a cleaver. For *The Count of Monte Cristo*, they flushed toilets in the studio bathroom to imitate oars splashing into the sea.

The music for each of the weekly programs was crucial to setting the mood—cheerful, mysterious, sinister. CBS's Bernard Herrmann collected appropriate music for the background and scene transitions, sometimes composing it himself.

Herrmann conducted his twenty-seven-piece orchestra during the live broadcasts each week, with Welles cueing when he wanted the music inserted. Though the two men argued, one Mercury actor recalled, "Bernard Herrmann knew exactly what Orson needed . . . and he delivered what Orson needed."

RENEWED

The Mercury's radio dramas weren't as popular as the programs featuring comedian Jack Benny, ventriloquist Edgar Bergen and his dummy Charlie McCarthy, or Major Bowes and his *Amateur Hour* performers. But Welles and his team attracted enough listeners during the summer for CBS to extend the program with thirteen new fall episodes. The broadcast time changed to Sunday nights at 8:00 p.m. when the network hoped to appeal to families and expand its audience.

With a one-hour program to write, rehearse, and perform every seven days, Welles

In 1938, *The Chase and Sanborn Hour* on NBC was the most popular Sunday night radio program. (left) Ventriloquist Edgar Bergen (1903–1978) and his wooden dummy Charlie McCarthy were two of the variety show's stars. Here they perform a skit with famous comedian W. C. Fields (1880-1946).

and Houseman were under—in Houseman's words—"conditions of soul- and health-destroying pressure." Once the fall radio season began in September, the pressure intensified. The two were already immersed in rehearsals for their second theatre season, opening in November. They physically couldn't keep up the pace of twenty-hour workdays.

To cope, they took on an experienced radio and theatre actor, Paul Stewart, as an associate producer. Each week, he directed the broadcast's preliminary rehearsals. That freed up Welles from directing duties until Sunday, the day of the broadcast.

To remove the writing load from Houseman, they hired a lanky thirty-six-year-old writer named Howard Koch. Koch wasn't the typical radio scriptwriter. Raised in Kingston, New York, a hundred miles up the Hudson River from Manhattan, he practiced law for several years in a New York City suburb.

But Koch hated the dreary, monotonous work. "I had to either learn the rules [of practicing law] or give up the game," he later said. "I decided that the game wasn't worth it." He wanted a more creative career instead, and he set out to develop the skills to become a playwright.

By the time Koch walked into the Mercury office in early fall of 1938, three of his plays had been produced. Still, he hadn't earned enough money as a playwright to support his family. Koch was willing to work for the modest salary the Mercury could afford. In early October, Houseman gave him a job.

Koch had to adjust to writing radio scripts, just as Houseman had. To give him a hand, Houseman loaned Koch his competent secretary, twenty-four-year-old Anne Froelick. She had grown up in Princeton, New Jersey. After dropping out of Smith College at nineteen, she moved to New York City. Froelick tried acting and

Howard Koch (1901–1995) was hired to write scripts for *The Mercury Theatre on the Air* in early fall 1938.

modeling without success before Houseman hired her to type scripts. In Houseman's words, she was a "tireless girl-of-all-work."

One night, Welles and Houseman met for dinner to choose a story for the last week in October. We ought to do some science fiction, they agreed. It would add variety to their season. In the past decade, science fiction had become popular in radio, comics, and film. Buck Rogers and Flash Gordon were two of the public's favorite space adventurers.

Houseman didn't enjoy the genre himself, but he knew his partner did. "What do you like, Orson?" he asked.

Welles had a few stories in mind. He and Houseman discussed each one. Finally, they settled on a novel written more than forty years earlier.

It turned out to be a fateful decision.

CHAPTER FOUR

BLOOD-RED PLANET

> "The world went in ignorance of one of the gravest dangers that ever threatened the human race." —*H. G. Wells*, The War of the Worlds

In late 1895, twenty-nine-year-old British author Herbert George Wells hatched the plot for a new story. He wrote a friend: "I'm doing the dearest little serial for Pearson's new magazine, in which I completely wreck and destroy Woking—killing my neighbours in painful and eccentric ways."

Before becoming a fiction writer, H. G. Wells had taught science and published two biology textbooks. Throughout his writing career, he stayed abreast of new ideas and discoveries by corresponding with researchers and reading scientific papers. Wells incorporated what he learned into his stories. With the publication of his novels *The Time Machine* and *The Island of Doctor Moreau* in the mid-1890s, he became known for his innovative scientific romances, today known as science fiction.

For his new tale, Wells was inspired by astronomers who proposed that life existed on Mars. (See sidebar, page 27.) He created his plot by imagining *What if . . . ?* What if an advanced civilization lived on Mars? And what if the planet were dying and those creatures had to find a new home?

Wells envisioned the Martians setting their sights

Herbert George (H. G.) Wells (1866–1946)

on their nearest neighbor, Earth, "a morning star of hope." He wrote: "Slowly and surely [they] drew their plans against us."

One day, the Martians landed a spaceship near London. Soon, the invaders had taken over the English countryside using hundred-foot-high fighting machines with spiderlike legs and "long, flexible, glittering tentacles."

ANNIHILATION

In his story, Wells described the Martians' bodies as "merely heads," "the size . . . of a bear," "about four feet in diameter," and covered with brown, oily skin. Each had "luminous" eyes and a mouth surrounded by sixteen "whip-like tentacles" resembling a "gray snake." The creatures communicated with each other telepathically.

Wells explained that the Martians nourished themselves by injecting a victim's blood directly into their veins. The invaders annihilated anyone who got in their way with a deadly Black Smoke and incinerating Heat-Rays. They cultivated a Red Weed that obliterated the landscape.

What if millions of terrified human survivors fled in a stampede, making their way to the sea where ships waited to evacuate them? "The main road was a boiling stream of people," Wells wrote, "a torrent of human beings rushing northward, one pressing on another."

And what if one of them, the story's narrator, was left behind to face the invaders?

Wells set the action a few years in the future—in the early twentieth century. By including the actual names of English towns and villages, he crafted fiction that seemed disturbingly real.

In 1897, *Pearson's Magazine* published *The War of the Worlds* as a series of nine monthly episodes. It was such a hit with British readers that an American magazine, *The Cosmopolitan*, carried the serial, too. The next year, Wells released it as a short novel.

Several elements of his story foretold the future. The lethal Black Smoke that left "men choking and writhing on the ground" portended the poison gases used two decades later during World War I. The Martians' destructive Heat-Rays resembled lasers, which weren't invented until the late 1950s. The fighting machines ("boilers on stilts") looked like taller forerunners of NASA's Apollo 11 lunar module from the 1969 Moon landing.

On the night of October 30, 1938, Wells—and the world—would find out how eerily accurate another of his prophecies had been.

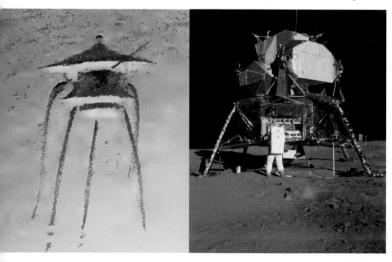

LEFT: Martian fighting machine from the 1906 edition of Wells's novel. RIGHT: NASA's lunar module *Eagle* and Apollo astronaut Edwin "Buzz" Aldrin on the Moon. On July 20, 1969, Aldrin and Neil Armstrong became the first humans to walk on the Moon.

MARTIANS?

The fourth planet from the Sun has stirred the imagination of humans for eons. Because of its blood-red appearance, both the Greeks and Romans named it after their god of war. Today, we use the Romans' *Mars*. The planet's color doesn't come from spilled blood of battle. It's due to the reddish rust of iron-containing rocks.

Depending on their orbits around the Sun, Mars and Earth move as close together as 35 million miles (56 million kilometers) or as far apart as 249 million miles (400 million kilometers). Whenever Mars came near, the early astronomers focused their telescopes on it in hopes of seeing surface details.

William Herschel (1738–1822), the astronomer from Great Britain who discovered Uranus, proposed in 1784 that the Mars environment could support intelligent life. Herschel was a respected scientist, and other astronomers accepted his idea.

In 1877, astronomer Giovanni Schiaparelli (1835–1910) drew a map of Mars based on the view through his telescope. He labeled the long straight lines he saw as canali, Italian for "channels." Although Schiaparelli was describing what he thought were natural structures, others mistakenly translated canali into "canal." To many, that could mean only one thing: Since canals on Earth are man-made, Mars's canals must have been built by intelligent creatures. Herschel had been right!

The notion of canals sparked the imagination of American amateur astronomer Percival Lowell (1855–1916), who claimed to have seen the lines through *his* telescope. He concluded that Mars was inhabited by a civilization far more advanced than Earth's. Lowell deduced that when the planet's oceans dried up, the Martians built a system of canals thousands of miles long to move water from the polar ice caps to dry areas.

"Certainly what we see hints at the existence of beings who are in advance of, not behind us, in the journey of life," Lowell wrote in his 1895 book. "What manner of beings they may be we lack the data even to conceive."

Most professional astronomers of the day were skeptical, believing the "canal lines" were optical illusions. But the vivid descriptions in the popular books by Lowell and his fervor in public lectures convinced millions of people for years to come that Mars was home to intelligent life.

H. G. Wells knew about Schiaparelli's canali and Lowell's advanced-civilization ideas. He didn't believe in brainy Martians, though he recognized the premise of a winning story. When *The War of the Worlds* was published just two years after Lowell's first book hit the shelves, Wells's scenario seemed entirely possible to his readers.

The Red Planet showing the Valles Marineris canyon system across the center. This Mars canyon is 8 kilometers (about 5 miles) deep and more than 3,000 kilometers (1,864 miles) long. The Grand Canyon in the United States is only 1.8 kilometers (about 1 mile) deep and less than 450 kilometers (about 280 miles) long. The three dark spots on the left side of the photo are volcanoes.

In May 1937, the German passenger airship *Hindenburg* carried ninety-seven people across the Atlantic Ocean from Germany. During its landing at Lakehurst Naval Air Station in Lakehurst, New Jersey, on the evening of May 6, it burst into flames and crashed. The accident killed thirty-five passengers and one person on the ground.

CHAPTER FIVE

PLOTTING THE INVASION

"No one . . . was very enthusiastic about it. But it seemed good programming."

—*John Houseman*

Houseman later admitted that neither he nor Welles remembered reading *The War of the Worlds*. No matter. They knew the storyline, and it had promise as a radio drama. Because the book was still in print, they assumed the public would be familiar with it, too.

The decision made, the men contacted H. G. Wells's legal representative in New York and bought the rights to adapt the novel into a radio play.

Orson Welles had a brainstorm. Let's update the story to the late 1930s, he suggested to Houseman. We'll develop the action using news bulletins.

This approach had been used on a few other radio dramas, and Welles thought it would increase the excitement and tension. Houseman went along with the idea.

During recent years, special newsflashes had interrupted regular radio programs to announce tragedies and disaster. The March 1932 kidnapping of aviator Charles Lindbergh's toddler son. The May 1937 deadly explosion of the *Hindenburg* airship in New Jersey. Hitler's March 1938 occupation of Austria. Listeners had been conditioned to pay close attention to these bulletins. Welles and Houseman hoped they could take advantage of this to hook their audience.

LIFE ON MARS?

To the two Mercury partners, a Martian invasion was pure fiction. They didn't grasp how plausible the idea was to some people.

In the 1920s, Guglielmo Marconi (the Nobel Prize–winning developer of the wireless telegraph) and other scientists claimed to have detected wireless signals from Mars. That news had further fueled the public's belief in intelligent life on the planet.

In December 1928, the *New York Times* interviewed an astronomer from the Harvard University Observatory. He reported seeing suspicious markings on Mars's surface just as Schiaparelli and Lowell had. "We can only explain them as the result of intelligent beings," Dr. William Pickering told the newspaper. He went on to say, "It is almost certain that Mars is" home to an advanced civilization and that the Martians might be sending signals to Earth.

Later, less than three years before Welles and Houseman decided to dramatize *The War of the Worlds*, the *New York Times* reported: "That there may be life on Mars is no longer denied by advanced astronomers."

Most scientists doubted that the Mars environment could support a humanlike life form. But for people who were unaware of that view, the reports about the mysterious planet kept alive the possibility that Martians existed.

FOOLS

At the end of the third week in October 1938, Houseman assigned *The War of the Worlds* to Howard Koch. It would be the writer's third script for *The Mercury Theatre on the Air*, and it would alter his life.

After Koch read the novel, he was dismayed. How could he adapt it the way Welles wanted? The only things he could use were the Martians' physical appearance and their weapons. In order to give the plot enough spark to grab a radio audience, he'd have to make so many changes to Wells's story that he'd be starting from scratch. He had less than a week to write an hour-long script!

Koch phoned Houseman, begging him to pick another story. "John, what are we going to do[?] This is terrible."

It's too late now, Houseman replied. Welles wants this one. Plow ahead.

Disheartened but resigned to the situation, Koch considered how to do the impossible. He had to shift the action from 1900 England to the late-1930s United States. Instead of destroying London and its suburbs, as the Martians did in the novel, Koch's aliens would create mayhem in the New York City area.

Following H. G. Wells's example, Koch planned to let the invaders wipe out real places. But which ones? On his day off that week, he drove up the Hudson River to see his ill father. As he returned to the city that evening, Koch pulled into a gas station and asked for a map so that he could pick out the doomed towns. The attendant handed him one of New Jersey.

When Koch reached his apartment on Manhattan's Riverside Drive, he unfolded the map. Where would the Martian spaceship land? Closing his eyes, he lowered his pencil. When he looked down, he had pinpointed Grovers Mill, a rural village in the center of New Jersey about fifty miles from New York City.

Koch liked the name's "authentic ring." The town wasn't far from Princeton University, which had an astronomical observatory. The H. G. Wells story featured an astronomer, and this gave Koch a chance to include one, too. He made Professor

Richard Pierson the central character. Orson Welles would voice the part.

Using the road map and novel to guide him, Koch tried to write the script Welles expected. He worked from dawn into the night in his apartment, scribbling his words in pencil onto a yellow pad. His assistant, Anne Froelick, typed up his handwritten pages, adding her own edits. When they finished about twenty pages, they gave them to Houseman for feedback.

By late Tuesday, both Koch and Froelick were discouraged. They doubted that American listeners would find the British story engaging, despite the updates.

"You can't do it!" Froelick exclaimed to Houseman over the phone. "Those old Martians are just a lot of nonsense. It's all too silly! We're going to make fools of ourselves! Absolute fools!"

Anne Froelick (1913–2010) in her early twenties, around the time she worked for The Mercury Theatre

WRITE. REWRITE. REPEAT.

Houseman knew there was no turning back. They had already announced *The War of the Worlds* as their next show. It would go on the air in five days, and they had to have a script ready for Thursday morning's rehearsal. Houseman trusted Koch's ability. The writer had hit a stumbling block, that's all. He just needed a nudge getting past it.

Houseman headed over to Koch's apartment. Working all night, he, Koch, and Froelick tackled the story, and together they made progress on the script. Once Houseman had them going again, he left the two to continue the work.

Throughout the next day, Koch feverishly wrote and rewrote, and Froelick edited and typed. Koch figured out how to orchestrate the battle in New Jersey, making "moves and countermoves between the invaders and the defenders." By Wednesday evening, they had a completed draft. It would require revisions, but they had made the deadline.

On Thursday, Paul Stewart took over, directing the first read-through at the CBS studio. Houseman was there to listen and take notes. The draft of the script was passed out to the Mercury actors chosen by Stewart, Welles, and Houseman. They were all first-rate, able to breathe life into their characters with little rehearsal. Unlike other *Mercury Theatre on the Air* episodes, this one had no parts for actresses. To shorten and adapt Wells's novel, Koch cut its female characters.

Sitting around a table, the actors read their lines aloud. A few played multiple

Rehearsal for the CBS radio program *Air Raid*, broadcast in October 1938. The show's writer, Archibald MacLeish (right; 1892–1982), looks on. Orson Welles (left) and Ray Collins (middle; 1889–1965) performed as actors. Both were part of the *Mercury Theatre on the Air* team that created the *War of the Worlds* program later that month.

parts. One read Welles's lines, because Orson was at a theatre several blocks away directing rehearsals for the latest Mercury play, *Danton's Death*.

Occasionally, someone suggested a change in the dialogue to make it sound more natural. An actor noticed that Koch had used a British line from Wells's story about hiding in the *drains*. The script was changed to the American word *sewers*.

They did the reading without music and sound effects. But Bernard Herrmann and a representative from the CBS sound department were there to prepare for their contributions at future rehearsals.

A staff member recorded the reading on an acetate disc. Welles insisted on this so that, he said, "I can hear it fresh aloud."

The actors thought the show would be a dud. "Nobody's going to believe this in a million years," said one. Another concluded that the Sunday show would be "lousy," even with music and sound effects. "Don't bother to listen," he told an acquaintance. "Probably bore you to death."

Late Thursday night, Welles, Houseman, and Stewart gathered in Welles's luxurious room at the St. Regis Hotel in Manhattan. After they listened to the recording, they came to the same conclusion as the actors. "We agreed it was a dull show," Houseman recalled.

Welles was blunt. It needs to be more thrilling. Beef up the eyewitness reports. Make the news bulletins seem real.

Having given his instructions, Welles hurried out of his hotel room to return to the *Danton's Death* rehearsal.

For the rest of the night, Houseman and Stewart labored over the script, adding details, sprucing up dialogue, and building suspense. Early Friday morning, they sent Koch their notes.

Over at Koch's apartment, he and Froelick made adjustments as their next deadline loomed. The CBS censors expected to see the script by Friday afternoon. Otherwise, they wouldn't give the go-ahead for the broadcast.

Even after several fifteen-hour days in a row, Koch wasn't sure they'd finish the revisions in time.

CHAPTER SIX

THE FINAL DAY

" Everybody likes a good story and I think radio is just about the best storyteller there is."

—*Orson Welles*

The CBS legal department wanted twenty-eight changes to Koch's revised script. The censors weren't happy about the authentic names. They couldn't risk a lawsuit brought by an offended organization. Besides that objection, they said, a few of the lines were too frightening. The graphic part in which people trample each other escaping the Martians would have to be cut.

Houseman and Koch resisted. They knew that one reason for the success of the original *War of the Worlds* novel was H. G. Wells's use of genuine names. They lost the argument. Names were changed, including the Columbia Broadcasting Building, the United States Weather Bureau, the New Jersey National Guard, and the famous St. Patrick's Cathedral in New York City. The panicked crowd scene was toned down.

Houseman had his doubts about how the show would turn out. But as he later said, "We had done our best and, after all, it was just another radio show."

TIME FOR TECH

By Saturday morning, the new script had been mimeographed and distributed to the cast and technical staff. Paul Stewart took charge of the rehearsal that day, working with the sound engineer to incorporate sound effects and music with the actors' voices.

The head of the CBS sound effects department in New York, Ora Nichols, opened her bag of science-fiction tricks. As inventor of more than one thousand radio effects, Nichols had created space-travel and alien sounds for the *Buck Rogers* radio show. She and her staff planned the best way to replicate the opening of the Martian spaceship in Grovers Mill, the bomber planes, a roaring cannon, and the gassing of New York City.

Sound effects experts Ora Nichols (1893–1951) and Frank Gow use their equipment to create just the right sounds for the radio program *The Ghost of Benjamin Sweet*, in August 1938. At the time, Nichols was head of CBS Radio's sound effects department and the only woman in the country working in the field. She began her sound effects career collaborating with her husband, Arthur Nichols, who invented the first sound machines for radio. He died in 1931.

For this show, the *Mercury* team would copy a familiar type of radio broadcast—a dance band performing in a ballroom. Bernard Herrmann and his orchestra experimented with various songs to play between newsflashes. During rehearsal, Herrmann and Stewart argued over the choice of music and its rhythm. The musician had a quick temper and his own ideas of how to do things.

One of the actors, Frank Readick, did extra homework for his role. He played Carl Phillips, a key character who provides eyewitness reports about the Martians' landing. Readick borrowed the 1937 recording made at the shocking scene of the *Hindenburg* disaster. He listened to the radio commentator's horrified voice as he

watches the passenger airship explode into flames. The man continues to record even as he is overcome with emotion and can barely speak. Readick played and replayed the recording until he was able to imitate the same reaction when his character sees the extraterrestrials emerge from their spaceship.

The Saturday technical rehearsal ended around six in the evening. Not long afterward, Orson Welles took a break from his *Danton's Death* rehearsal to call the studio. Everyone had gone home except one of the sound effects men.

Welles asked him how the show was going.

"Very dull. Very dull," he replied. "It'll put 'em to sleep."

This wasn't good news. Welles realized how much work he'd have to do at the next day's rehearsal to whip the show into shape.

WELLES ON THE PODIUM

Early Sunday afternoon, Welles showed up at Studio One, on the twentieth floor of CBS's Madison Avenue building. In a few short hours, the show would go live on the air.

He took his position on a raised podium in the middle of the studio. Welles wore headphones so that he could hear all the voices, music, and sound effects. As director, his job was to signal the actors when it was time for them to read their lines. He cued sound effects and music to fade in and out.

In front of him were his microphone and a music stand holding the script marked with cues and timings from the previous rehearsal. As the afternoon went on, more marks and notes would be added.

The actors gathered around a nearby microphone where they could watch Welles's hand signals. While reading their lines, they had to be careful not to rustle the script's pages. Otherwise, the microphone would pick it up. They kept their heads steady and mouths aimed at the microphone so that the volume of their voices didn't fluctuate.

The Mercury team broadcasts a *Mercury Theatre on the Air* show from the CBS studio. Actors circle the microphone in front of the control room. Orson Welles directs from a raised platform (in the middle of the photograph). Conductor Bernard Herrmann (1911–1975) sits on the right with his orchestra, out of the photograph frame, in front of him. In the foreground, the sound effects team waits for the cue to use their equipment and discs containing prerecorded sounds.

To Welles's left, the orchestra sat on chairs facing Herrmann, who was ready to conduct when Welles cued music. The sound effects team operated their equipment from a spot where they could see Welles, too. They played some of the sounds from 78-rpm (revolutions per minute) acetate records. They created others live using their collection of paraphernalia.

Behind the control room glass, Houseman monitored the rehearsal so that he could give his impressions to Welles. He was joined by Davidson Taylor, the CBS production supervisor for the *Mercury Theatre* program. The sound engineer was there, too, taking notes about when and how to adjust the sound. Usually, Paul Stewart was in the control booth. But for this show, he had to go into the studio twice to play two minor roles as announcers.

Like most rehearsals run by Welles, this one was wild. He repeatedly cursed, complaining that he had to present "so silly a show." As the afternoon sped by and the clock ticked down to airtime, Welles became more frenzied. Throwing his arms around, he made changes to the previously rehearsed script, delivered his own lines as Professor Richard Pierson, and impatiently screamed instructions at everyone else.

A *Mercury* actor described how Welles operated: "He could give hand signals with the hand that had [his] pipe, or the other hand, it didn't matter which, and Orson was in control, in command, and he loved this."

Houseman portrayed his partner's style: "Sweating, howling, disheveled, and singlehanded he wrestled with chaos and time."

Welles added back a section cut from Koch's earlier draft, a speech from the secretary of war. He wanted the comments identified as coming from the secretary of the interior, less likely to upset the nervous CBS censors. Welles assigned Kenny Delmar to that part, knowing the actor did a spot-on imitation of President Franklin Roosevelt.

Between March 1933 and October 1938, Roosevelt had broadcast thirteen fireside chats about the state of the nation. The public knew his voice well. Several years

In 1937, President Franklin Roosevelt (1882–1945) delivers one of his fireside chats, broadcast on the radio nationwide.

before, the White House requested—and broadcasters agreed—that the president should not be imitated on the radio because it confused listeners. On orders from his CBS bosses, Delmar wasn't supposed to do his impersonation except in special situations with permission from the White House.

Welles, who was well aware of this, smiled at the actor. "Oh Kenny, you know what I want."

Houseman later admitted, "That was the only naughty thing we did that night. Everything else was just good radio."

DRESS REHEARSAL

Dress rehearsal began with less than two hours to go. This was the final chance to blend the actors, sound effects, and music. It was the last time to lengthen or shorten the show. They would be broadcasting live, and the show had to fit within the one-hour schedule.

Houseman watched the electric clock on the studio wall, fretting that Welles had slowed down the beginning of the program too much. The weather report seemed tedious. The interview about science felt tiresome. "There [will] not be a listener left," he warned Welles.

Welles responded by slowing down the first part even more and stretching out the musical numbers. To stay under the sixty-minute mark, he cut lines from the script's ending. The changes shifted the station break ten minutes later than its normal point halfway through the show.

As the turmoil and yelling continued, the minutes slipped by. "How we got on the air each week was a miracle," Paul Stewart recalled.

Finally, after an intense afternoon, Houseman saw that the show had magically come together. Welles had calmed down, and "a strange fever seemed to invade the studio—part childish mischief, part professional zeal."

It was 7:59 p.m. Eastern Time in CBS's Studio One.

With a minute to go before airtime, the studio floor was cluttered with the debris of nearly eight hours of a frantic, stormy rehearsal. The air was stale and smelled of sandwiches and coffee. The lights were bright.

The actors cleared their throats. The musicians brought their instruments to position.

Welles took a long gulp of pineapple juice, adjusted his headphones, and raised his hand to give the first cue.

CHAPTER SEVEN

THE ATTACK

" It was the beginning of the rout of civilization, of the massacre of mankind."

—*H. G. Wells,* The War of the Worlds

At the cue, Dan Seymour announces Orson Welles and *The Mercury Theatre on the Air* performing H. G. Wells's *The War of the Worlds*. Bernard Herrmann's orchestra begins to play the *Mercury*'s theme song, Tchaikovsky's Piano Concerto no. 1 in B-flat Minor. After thirty seconds, Seymour presents Welles, star of the program.

In his deep, expressive voice, Welles introduces the radio play. He speaks for almost two minutes as the story's narrator. His words are nearly identical to the start of the novel. Earth was being watched from across space by those with "envious eyes" and sinister plans. The time has changed from Wells's early twentieth century to 1939— one year in the future.

After Welles's introduction, an announcer reads a detailed (and fake) weather report from the Government Weather Bureau. When he finishes, he turns the program over to the Meridian Room in New York City's Hotel Park Plaza (also fake).

Welles cues Bernard Herrmann, and the CBS orchestra plays a Spanish tango. As this music continues in the background, the Meridian Room announcer introduces Ramón Raquello and his orchestra.

So far, about three minutes have passed since the broadcast began. The show has been unhurried and leisurely, as Welles rehearsed. The weather report was routine—even boring—with details about air pressure, wind speeds, and temperature maximums and minimums.

SPECIAL BULLETIN

In the middle of the song "La Cumparsita," the music fades as a news announcer cuts in with a special bulletin. His report explains that a professor at a Chicago observatory has spotted several gas explosions on Mars. The announcer uses the same scientific words that H. G. Wells added to his novel: "incandescent gas" and "spectroscope." They make the bulletin seem genuine.

In the first hint that radio time isn't moving at the same speed as reality, the announcer says that the Chicago observation occurred at 7:40 p.m., Central Time. In the living rooms of listeners, clocks won't reach this time until thirty-six minutes in the future.

The news bulletin ends, and Spanish music from the Meridian Room returns to the air. It continues for about twenty seconds, followed by applause. As the clapping dies down, Ramón Raquello's orchestra begins "Stardust," a popular tune.

Welles lets the music go on for almost half a minute before cueing Herrmann to fade out. He points to the news announcer actor, who breaks in with a second bulletin: The Government Meteorological Bureau has asked observatories to watch for more explosions on Mars. The announcer adds that the station will soon carry an interview with the well-known astronomer Professor Richard Pierson.

Then it's back to "Stardust" at the Meridian Room.

After twenty seconds of music, the announcer interrupts a third time to introduce commentator Carl Phillips, who will conduct the interview.

Actor Frank Readick, as Carl Phillips, greets the radio audience. He says that he is at the Princeton Observatory in New Jersey. His voice echoes as if he is in a cavernous room. A clock ticks in the background. An early scene from the Wells's novel also included a steadily ticking observatory clock.

Beginning his interview, Phillips asks Professor Pierson about those Martian stripes visible through a telescope.

Orson Welles, as Pierson, speaks with authority. "Not canals, I can assure you, . . . although that's the popular conjecture of those who imagine Mars to be inhabited." His voice has a condescending edge. No, he continues, the stripes are due to Mars's atmosphere.

To listeners uninterested in astronomy, the interview promises to be dry.

So, asks Phillips, you don't think there's intelligent life on Mars?

"I'd say the chances against it are a thousand to one," replies Pierson. He notes that Mars is forty million miles away from Earth.

"A safe enough distance," the commentator says, chuckling.

MYSTERIOUS OBJECT

The ticking continues.

Professor Pierson is handed a telegram from the National History Museum in New York (again, fake). The astronomer permits Carl Phillips to share its contents with the radio audience.

According to the telegram, an earth-rattling shock occurred near Princeton at 9:15 p.m. Eastern Time.

In the homes of East Coast listeners, it is about 8:09 p.m. Time is speeding up, and with it, the pace of the action.

Could this have anything to do with the explosions on Mars? Phillips wants to know. Professor Pierson says no. He thinks it is likely a large meteorite.

Phillips thanks the professor for the ten-minute interview. He sends the program back to the New York studio.

In real time, the interview lasted three minutes.

From his podium, Orson Welles cues music. A piano fades in with a slow melody. The music continues for ten seconds.

Then, for the fourth time since the broadcast began, the news announcer interrupts with a special bulletin: An astronomer at McGill University in Canada has just seen three more explosions on Mars.

In an urgent voice, the announcer alerts listeners to a newsflash from Trenton, New Jersey: "At 8:50 p.m. a huge, flaming object, believed to be a meteorite, fell on a farm in the neighborhood of Grovers Mill, New Jersey." He tells the audience that people saw the flash from hundreds of miles away. Commentator Carl Phillips is on the way to Grovers Mill from Princeton to report more details.

Welles cues music again as the program supposedly switches to Brooklyn's Hotel Martinet. Herrmann's orchestra imitates a swing band's jazzy rhythms and brassy sound. After about twenty seconds, Welles signals for him to silence the instruments.

The news announcer breaks in. "We take you now to Grovers Mill, New Jersey."

A crowd buzzes with excitement. Sirens blare.

In another hint of warped time, Phillips explains that he and Professor Pierson have traveled eleven miles from Princeton to Grovers Mill in ten minutes. Actually, less than a minute has elapsed since Phillips " left" the Princeton Observatory.

Talking rapidly, Carl Phillips describes what he sees at the farm where the flaming object landed. It was no meteor. A pale yellow cylinder, thirty yards in diameter, is partially buried in a huge pit. People are crowding around it, he reports. The police try to stop them from getting any closer. Men shout in the background.

The cylinder, thirty yards in diameter, buried in a huge pit

Phillips spots the farmer who owns the land. "Mr. Wilmuth, would you please tell the radio audience as much as you remember?" He urges Wilmuth to stand near the microphone and to speak louder.

Wilmuth, played by Ray Collins, eagerly tells his story. He had his radio on and heard the professor discussing Mars. Then he heard hissing. "I seen a kinda greenish streak and then zingo! Somethin' smacked the ground."

To listeners, it sounds like an authentic news interview with a person who has never spoken into a microphone before.
The program has been on the air for thirteen minutes.

Phillips ends the interview and resumes his report. Hundreds of cars have arrived at the farm, parking along the road and in a field. Their headlights shine on the pit. Trying to control the crowd, angry police officers call out. People stand along the pit's edge, staring down at the cylinder.

LOOK OUT!

Phillips mentions a strange hum coming from inside the object. He moves his microphone closer. Radio listeners hear a scraping sound. Phillips asks Professor Pierson whether he'd still say this is a meteor.

"I don't know what to think," replies Pierson/Welles. "The metal casing is definitely extraterrestrial."

Suddenly, Phillips calls out, "Something's happening!" The cylinder top is unscrewing.

Bystanders holler, "Keep back...! Keep back!"

Plunk. The top drops to the ground.

It's pandemonium as the startled crowd reacts.

"This is the most terrifying thing I have ever witnessed, . . ." Phillips says. "Something's wriggling out of the shadow like a gray snake." Horrified, he describes the creature the way H. G. Wells did in his novel—the leathery skin, the tentacles, the quivering mouth. "I can hardly force myself to keep looking at it, it's so awful."

Phillips tells the audience to wait while he moves to a better location.

Piano music returns.

Time seems to drag until listeners hear Phillips's voice again, but really, just ten seconds go by.

Breathlessly, Phillips reports that he has moved behind a stone wall. The crowd has backed away from the monster in the pit. Sirens scream as more police arrive.

A low-pitched hum breaks through the din, followed by an electronic beep, like a warning signal. *Bleep. Bleep. Bleep. Bleep.* It grows louder.

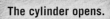
The cylinder opens.

The monster shoots a flash of fire toward the crowd.

As Phillips, Frank Readick describes the scene, imitating the frantic *Hindenburg* commentator. Stammering at times, he speaks so fast that his words slur together. "A humped shape is rising out of the pit." He sees a flash of fire shot at three policemen. "Good Lord, they're turning into flame!"

A man shrieks. Others wail in pain.

The field and woods are burning. The flames are within twenty yards of Phillips's position. He cries out, "It's coming this way."

The radio goes dead.

For six seconds, there is total silence. To radio listeners, it feels more like six minutes. An eternity.

HEAT RAY

At last, Orson Welles cues the next line in the script.

The voice of the studio announcer informs the audience that the network has lost the connection to Grovers Mill.

Soft, serene piano music plays for ten seconds. By now, the piano has become an omen of looming disaster.

The announcer abruptly interrupts the music to report on a telephone message received from Grovers Mill. "At least forty people ... lie dead ..., their bodies burned and distorted." The extraterrestrial attacker has returned to the pit.

The commander of the New Jersey state militia comes on the air. In a measured tone, he announces martial law in the counties surrounding Grovers Mill. The militia will proceed to the area and help evacuate homes.

After the commander's remarks, contact is established with Professor Pierson, who

The Martian heat ray sets fires near the pit.

witnessed the carnage before finding shelter at a farmhouse. The transmission is full of static, apparently caused by the makeshift connection.

Pierson describes the creature's weapon, a heat ray. It's clear to him that the invaders possess "scientific knowledge far in advance of our own." In explaining the

The Martian machines attack.

destructive power source, he uses technical phrases from the H. G. Wells novel: "absolute nonconductivity . . . parallel beam . . . polished parabolic mirror."

When Pierson finishes, a studio announcer shares the shocking news. "The charred body of Carl Phillips has been identified."

After several more bulletins about the situation, listeners hear the voice of an officer at the New Jersey militia's field headquarters near Grovers Mill. The captain explains that the cylinder is surrounded by soldiers carrying machine guns and rifles. With all this firepower, he says, there is no reason to worry. He talks for more than a minute, assuring listeners that the enemy won't be able to resist the militia's weapons.

Motion on top of the cylinder catches the captain's eye. "It's something moving . . . kind of shieldlike affair rising up out of the cylinder. . . . It's going higher and higher." Standing on metal legs, it rises above the trees. "Hold on!" he yells.

There is sudden silence as the transmission is cut off.

Welles waits five seconds before cueing the announcer.

"Ladies and gentlemen, I have a grave announcement to make. Incredible as it may seem . . . those strange beings who landed in the Jersey farmlands tonight are the vanguard of an invading army from the planet Mars."

The announcer continues: In the battle at Grovers Mill, 7,000 soldiers fought the Martians. All but 120 were mowed down, "crushed and trampled to death under the metal feet of the monster, or burned to cinders by its heat ray."

The deadly heat ray mows down military resistance.

49

A Martian tripod on the move through the countryside.

Many hours had gone by since the Martian cylinder first landed in Grovers Mill. Less than half an hour passed in radio listeners' living rooms. Welles had manipulated the audience's perception of time by dragging out the program's beginning and then accelerating once the newsflashes started.

The announcer introduces the secretary of the interior. Actor Kenny Delmar speaks, perfectly mimicking President Franklin Roosevelt. "I shall not try to conceal the gravity of the situation that confronts the country." In a comforting yet forceful voice, he urges calm. The enemy, he says, is "confined to a comparatively small area," and the military will prevent them from escaping.

IN THE CONTROL ROOM

While Delmar was finishing the secretary of interior speech, the phone rang in the Studio One control room. Davidson Taylor answered it. As the CBS supervisor listened, he pinched his lips. Hanging up, he rushed from the room.

John Houseman wondered what happened. He thought the show was going extremely well.

A few minutes later, Taylor returned. Houseman saw that the color had drained from his face.

Distraught, he turned to Houseman. They had a problem. The world had gone mad.

CHAPTER EIGHT

PANIC

"The Martians are coming!" —*H. G. Wells,* The War of the Worlds

"Martians have landed . . ." —*New Jersey resident*

The phones started ringing at CBS's New York headquarters as soon as the creature emerged from its cylinder. Callers were hysterical. "The Martians are invading! What do we do?"

The Mercury Theatre on the Air was being carried that night by dozens of stations throughout the United States, and the calls came from all over. The CBS telephone operators were soon overwhelmed. They politely told people that they were listening to a dramatic show, not news. "Don't panic," they said. "There are no invaders."

William Paley, the president of CBS, was home playing cards when his office phoned him. "A terrible thing has happened," he was told. "The whole country [is] bursting wide open."

DIALING FOR HELP

CBS headquarters wasn't the only place that anxious listeners called. In 1938, there was no 911. To get help in an emergency, people contacted their local telephone operator. Those who had dial phones dialed zero. Customers still without a dial picked up their phone's receiver, and an operator answered.

In Princeton, New Jersey, operators responded to screaming and crying callers. Had they'd seen the Martians? How bad was the destruction? Were bodies lying around the streets?

A man told a New York City operator that people were planning to kill their children before the Martians could get them.

In Missoula, Montana, an operator handled calls from customers begging her to connect their phone to family members. They wanted to say "I love you" one last time before the world ended.

Because they were on duty, the operators hadn't heard the radio program and didn't know what was happening. But they had been trained to stay calm and help

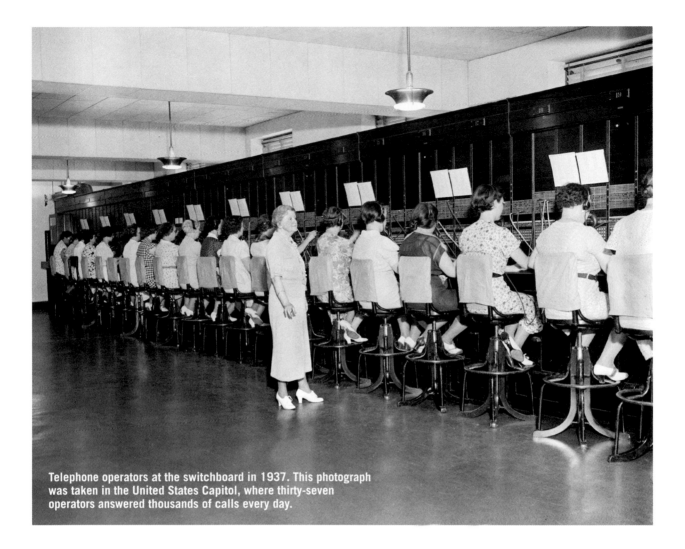

Telephone operators at the switchboard in 1937. This photograph was taken in the United States Capitol, where thirty-seven operators answered thousands of calls every day.

the best they could. As soon as operators learned the truth, they reassured callers that the crisis was just part of a radio show.

In one South Dakota community, however, the local operator believed the Martians *had* invaded. She felt it was her responsibility to call as many homes as possible, warning that the extraterrestrials were on the way.

Rumors spread as friends and family shared news of the attack, alarming people who had not been listening to the broadcast. To confirm the story, some phoned their local newspapers, radio stations, or the police. At first, callers asked whether there had been a meteor strike in New Jersey. As the broadcast continued, the inquiries became more fearful and mentioned Martian heat-ray attacks, explosions, and mass casualties.

Before the night ended, the *New York Times* received nearly nine hundred calls about the invasion. The *New York Daily News* reported more than one thousand.

TOO CLOSE FOR COMFORT

The real Grovers Mill was a rural area too small to have a post office. Several local farmers heard the *Mercury Theatre* broadcast. Ready to defend their community, they grabbed their shotguns and drove to the pond near the mill. When they arrived, they found no hundred-foot Martian tripods. Only a few other curious people.

Two miles from Grovers Mill, sixteen-year-old Lolly was playing the piano at a youth church meeting. Someone came in, yelling, "Martians have landed in Grover's Mill." The group scattered, and Lolly ran down the road to her home. When she burst in, frightened and upset, her mother had no idea what was wrong.

Ingeborg was doing the dishes in northern New Jersey when she switched on the radio. Not long after 8:00 p.m., she heard a newscaster say that a Martian cylinder had landed in Grovers Mill. The lights in her house *had* flickered at 7:30 that evening . . . and wasn't the announcer talking about towns she knew well? Gathering up her photograph albums, Ingeborg told her husband to drive them to safety—if that was even possible!

SCARED ON CAMPUS

At Saint Elizabeth College, in Morristown, New Jersey, a woman raced down a dormitory hall screaming, "A rocket is coming from Mars. We're all going to be killed!" Students became hysterical. One group gathered to pray. Others froze, unable to decide what to do.

Panicked students in Georgia and North Carolina rushed to phones to call home. In Oregon, university fraternity brothers gathered around a radio, "spellbound" and "scared to death."

At West Virginia University, students cried in each other's arms, phoned their parents to say good-bye forever, and hid in the dormitory basement. One student ran to warn the town of the Martian attack.

At Oberlin College in Ohio, a young woman watched the people in her dorm become unglued as they listened to the program. She wondered why they didn't have the sense to verify the newsflashes by switching to a different station.

A college student and his roommate were driving south from New York State to their home in New Jersey. Suddenly, they heard about the destruction on the car radio. Certain that their "friends and families were all dead," the driver steered the car around and sped north as fast as it would go. "All I could think of was being burned alive," he admitted later. "I thought the whole human race was going to be wiped out."

LIVES IN DANGER

Soon after eight o'clock, the telephone rang at Frederick's home in Watervliet, New York. Turn on your radio, his friend said. Something horrible is happening in New Jersey. The family put on CBS. When they heard President Roosevelt (or so they believed) speak about the emergency, Frederick and his wife knew they had to protect their children. They lived close to New Jersey and had to get away, though they had no idea where they'd go.

In East Douglas, Massachusetts, John tuned to NBC's variety show *The Chase and Sanborn Hour* and listened for a while. But he didn't like the singing, so he twirled the dial through the stations, searching for a more entertaining program. When he settled on CBS, Carl Phillips was interviewing Farmer Wilmuth. As John listened, the situation became more dire. The country was in danger. He hurried to tell the other families in his building. Then he ran outside to look for the Martian attack machines.

Dean and his wife of Highland, Wisconsin, were listening to dance music on their radio when it was interrupted by the newsflash about a Mars disturbance. As the reports continued, their concern grew. "I sat on the edge of the davenport and began to shake all over," Dean later recalled. The couple was sure that the Martians would soon land in Wisconsin.

It was shortly after five o'clock in Centralia, Washington, when Edith turned on *The Mercury Theatre*, live from New York City. She knew something was wrong as soon as she heard the first news bulletin. Her newspaper listed *The Pickwick Papers* as the *Mercury's* presentation that evening (evidently a misprint). What she heard on her radio was definitely

A Michigan couple listens to a radio broadcast in 1939.

not the Charles Dickens story. The description of the destruction horrified her. Edith had relatives in New Jersey, and she was worried about their safety. Remembering the Lindbergh kidnapping and the *Hindenburg* catastrophe, she thought with dismay, "So much has happened in N.J."

S. L. and his wife of Los Angeles, California, tuned to *The Mercury Theatre* in time to hear the newsflash about the meteor. They were shocked when the Martians killed so many people. They never imagined it was possible. Yet here were statements by "Professors, National Guard Officers, Scientists and the Secretary of the Interior."

In Sanford, Florida, a group of friends—alerted by a neighbor who was listening to the program—gathered together to follow the awful news. One woman's daughter lived in New York. What would happen to her? As the chilling reports continued, everyone was astounded. How can this be happening—Mars defeating us!

CHAPTER NINE

"WRECKAGE"

" People were fighting savagely . . .
being trampled and crushed."

—*H. G. Wells*, The War of the Worlds

In the Studio One control room, Davidson Taylor told John Houseman about the rattled calls to CBS. "You've got to stop the show." Taylor went on: People believe this is real. We have to explain that it's a play.

"No! No! Never! Never! You can't ruin the show," Houseman argued, blocking him from entering the studio and interrupting Welles.

Reluctantly, Taylor agreed to hold off until the station break. But that was several long minutes away.

ON THE AIR

At the microphone, Kenny Delmar, as the secretary of the interior, has finished his speech.

An announcer returns. "Bulletins too numerous to read are piling up." He mentions actual names of towns and cities from where the reports are coming.

The Martian enemy advances.

A tripod is brought down by an Army gun shell.

The aim of the enemy, he says, "is to crush resistance, paralyze communication, and disorganize human society." Heat rays have destroyed power lines, blacking out communication with parts of New Jersey, the announcer adds. Highways are jammed as people flee. Astronomers think that regular outbursts continue on the Mars surface and more cylinders will soon land on Earth.

The audience is patched in to the direct reports from a field artillery battery in New Jersey's Watchung Mountains. Soldiers are in the middle of an attack. Radio listeners hear them coughing and gasping as they are overcome by the invaders' poisonous black smoke.

The sound switches to a lieutenant aboard an Army bombing plane over New Jersey while he speaks with his commander on the ground. The lieutenant spots six tripod fighting machines, one partially damaged from an Army gun shell. The Martians are turning east toward New York City.

He describes his eight bombers circling the machines, getting closer and closer, ready to attack. Suddenly, he shouts, "Green flash! They're spraying us with flame!"

The plane spirals out of control.

Abruptly, the transmission cuts off. Radio listeners hear nothing for several seconds.

Then a ham-radio operator from Bayonne, New Jersey, breaks the silence: "Eight army bombers in engagement with enemy tripod machines. . . . Engines incapacitated by heat ray. All crashed."

Another operator reports from Newark, New Jersey: "Poisonous black smoke pouring in. . . . Gas masks useless." He reads off the best highway escape routes.

A radio announcer's voice returns, explaining that he's on the Broadcasting Building roof in New York City. In the background, church bells toll, warning the public to evacuate because the Martians are coming. He reports that three million people have left the city during the past two hours.

Once again, listeners are given a clue that the program's time is passing faster than reality. Only about thirty-five minutes have elapsed since it began.

The Martians use a heat ray to destroy everything in their path.

Martian machines cross the river.

"Artillery, air force, everything wiped out," the announcer says, trying to contain his emotions. "This may be the last broadcast."

He goes on to describe the harbor full of crowded boats leaving the docks. Ship horns bellow in the background.

He spots the enemy approaching from the west. Five tripod machines. One wades across the Hudson River. The other four follow.

The announcer is handed a news bulletin, and he reads it to the audience. Martian cylinders have landed throughout the United States—in Buffalo, Chicago, St. Louis.

The tripods come ashore on the west side of Manhattan. "This is the end now," the announcer says hopelessly.

As deadly smoke fills the streets, thousands of people try to escape it, but fall "like flies." Some reach the East River, where they jump in "like rats."

The smoke is spreading ever faster, approaching the announcer's perch on the Broadcasting Building roof. He chokes. He can no longer speak. His body falls with a thud.

The radio audience has heard yet another on-the-air death.

For nearly half a minute, the only sound is the mournful cry of ship horns fading away.

The silence ends with the voice of a ham-radio operator trying to contact others. "Isn't there anyone on the air? Isn't there anyone . . . ?"

Nobody answers.

At forty minutes past the hour, the *Mercury Theatre*'s Dan Seymour announces to the audience that they are listening to a presentation of H. G. Wells's *The War of the Worlds* on CBS Radio.

An intermission lasts about twenty seconds, during which stations across the country can make announcements.

Tripods invade the city.

AT LAST, THE STATION BREAK

During the brief break, on instructions from CBS officials, Orson Welles was told to step out of character and explain to the audience that the program was a play. Welles saw no need to make such a change in the script. He and the other actors in the studio remained unaware of the commotion outside.

Alerted by phone calls to its offices, the Associated Press (AP) sent out a message to the country's news organizations informing them that the CBS broadcast was a fictional radio drama. Smelling a story, reporters and photographers from New York's newspapers raced to the CBS building.

BACK TO THE SHOW

The program resumes with the CBS announcer introducing the second part of *The War of the Worlds*. Herrmann's orchestra plays somber music.

Welles's voice returns as Professor Pierson, recounting the days since the great Martian attack. He has seen the Martians feed on humans, and he has hidden to survive. He moves north, trying to evade the tripods.

In Newark, New Jersey, Pierson comes upon a man crouched in a doorway. It is the first person he has seen alive since he went into hiding in the empty Grovers Mill farmhouse.

There are no more fake news bulletins. The play takes the form of a narrated story with two characters. It is much less exciting than the first part, but many listeners have already been spooked.

The stranger, played by actor Carl Frank, had been in the militia. "They wrecked the greatest country in the world," he tells Pierson. "We're done. We're licked."

Pierson replies with a line out of H. G. Wells: "We're eatable ants."

The stranger plans to live underground in the subways and sewers, recruiting survivors. Together, they will gain control of the fighting machines, defeat the Martians, and take over the world.

Pierson decides he's better off on his own. He makes his way through the Holland Tunnel under the Hudson River into Manhattan. Walking toward Times Square, he passes bodies in the street and smells death.

Then he spots the shining top of a Martian tripod ahead. Ignoring the danger, he runs into Central Park and scrambles up a hill to get a better look.

He sees them. Nineteen Martian machines stand in a line, their metal arms dangling. A flock of blackbirds circles. "Stark and silent, lay the Martians," Pierson says, "with the hungry birds pecking and tearing brown shreds of flesh from their dead bodies."

Text continues on page 66

A tripod haunts an empty town.

Dead Martians lie next to their abandoned tripod machines.

The Earth's bacteria had infected the extraterrestrial invaders, who lacked immunity to them.

Koch had used H. G. Wells's nineteenth-century ending. Inspired by the new idea of germ theory, Wells imagined microbes killing off his Martians.

BOO!

With less than a minute to go, Herrmann's orchestra launches into a dramatic finale, marking the end of the radio play.

Orson Welles returns as himself. He tells listeners that what they have just heard was "the Mercury Theatre's own radio version of dressing up in a sheet and jumping out of a bush and saying 'Boo!' . . . We annihilated the world before your very ears."

He bids the audience good-bye with his final words: "If your doorbell rings and nobody's there, that was no Martian . . . it's Hallowe'en."

As the hour drew to a close in Studio One, the *Mercury* mischief-makers were about to find out how much trouble they had stirred up.

CHAPTER TEN

IT'S ALL OVER

"We all felt the world was coming to an end."

—Radio listener

On the other side of the radio, hearts were pounding. To many listeners, the *Mercury*'s Halloween program had been far too real.

TERRIFIED

In Newark, New Jersey, Mrs. Garrison stared at her radio, stunned. During the broadcast, her neighbors on Maril Place had run outside to search the sky. She was sure it was the end for all of them when she heard the ham operator warning that poison smoke had reached South Street, near her home. Even after the program was over and she learned the truth, she couldn't recover from the shock.

In Summit, New Jersey, sixteen-year-old Jo heard about the Martian heat ray from her alarmed neighbor. Grabbing her coat and her mother, Jo ran to her uncle's apartment. She smelled the invaders' deadly black smoke, and it made her cough. "Oh Mother," she cried, "we are all going to die tonight." When they arrived at her uncle's home, he told them that the heat ray and black smoke were just part of an Orson Welles story. He laughed, but Jo was too upset to see humor in what had happened to her.

Estelle and John of New York City turned on their radio about ten minutes after eight o'clock. It sounded as if they had tuned to a news broadcast. As they listened, "one horrible thing after another happened." They knew they'd be trapped by the gas and smoke if they stayed in Manhattan. The couple hurried to the railroad station, boarding a train headed for Hartford, Connecticut . . . which was as far away as they could get.

Taking their seats, they felt lucky to have beaten the mob that would follow once everyone learned about the Martian invasion. When they told their fellow passengers about the crisis, someone suggested it had to do with Orson Welles. Estelle found a newspaper in the train car and checked the radio listings. Sure enough. They had been listening to *The Mercury Theatre*. Estelle and John felt foolish. Worse, they had spent their money on one-way tickets to Hartford and had to borrow train fare to get home.

Thomas B. and his family were driving from Long Island to New York City. The car radio was tuned to dance music when a newsflash interrupted. Soon, there were more bulletins and the secretary of the interior's speech. Upon hearing that the "fearful monster" was crossing into Manhattan, Thomas steered off the highway to find a telephone. Hoping he could get more information about the best escape route, he called New York City's police headquarters. The entire thing is fake, the police told him. That did little to calm Thomas's passengers, who had "suffered agony."

In Ithaca, New York, Hugh had turned to the *Mercury* program late, too. As he listened to the startling news bulletins, he worried about the fate of his family. His wife was traveling on a train in New Jersey; his son lived in Trenton; his daughter lived just outside New York City. "In this day of glaring headlines the shock was tremendous," he said later.

In a town near Philadelphia, William and his wife switched on *The Mercury Theatre* several minutes after it began. They didn't realize they were listening to a drama. As the situation worsened, they took out a map to find how far away Grovers Mill was. Their anxiety grew when the Martians went on the move.

Taking no chances, they gathered all the money in the house, bundled up their baby, and prepared to leave town for a safer location. Then they heard the announcement that it had been a play. The two realized they'd been "fools together scared to death."

Stella of Arbon, Idaho, was a regular *Mercury Theatre* listener. When she tuned in the program that Sunday night, the first thing she heard was that an object had fallen in New Jersey. As the newsflashes continued, she became more unnerved. After poison gas killed the announcer, she switched the radio off. It was more than she could take. Stella resigned herself to death. She didn't learn the truth until she drove to her uncle's house to find comfort, and he told her it was a play.

Immediately after George and his family of Sheboygan, Wisconsin, dialed the radio to *The Mercury Theatre*, a newsflash came on. They assumed the evening's regular program had been canceled because of the invasion. Petrified, George's wife cried, "I bet thats [sic] something from Germany." George was trembling, and their two daughters were visibly disturbed by the report. When they learned it had been a dramatization, the family was thankful. "For a Halloween scare," said George later that night, "it couldn't be beat."

At Kansas University, fraternity brothers gathered around the radio. As the Martian invasion continued, they became more frightened. Two of their friends decided to play a trick on the unhinged group. As news broke that the Martians had reached the Midwest, the pranksters lit firecrackers in the basement and flicked off the electricity. One of them later remarked, "I never have seen such a scared bunch of college boys in my life."

ANGRY

Shortly after nine o'clock, Esther of Providence, Rhode Island, switched off her radio and rolled a sheet of paper into her typewriter. Fuming, she composed a letter to CBS.

As soon as the broadcast ended, listeners sat down to compose letters of complaint or praise. Most of the letters were typed. This 1940 photograph shows a woman using a portable typewriter of the time.

The network should be banned from presenting such a program ever again, she wrote. "If you and your cast had just gone through the horrors of the hurricane [in September 1938], lost your homes and friends, you would be down on your knees thanking God for saving you."

Outside New York City, Gerta was putting her son to bed when her neighbor knocked on the door. Hurry! the agitated woman exclaimed. You have to hear what's on the radio. Gerta listened to the announcement from Washington. She was concerned about the reports of black smoke and gas near places she recognized. It could be true, she thought. Hadn't they said on the news a few years ago that strange signals were coming from Mars and that it had canals?

When Gerta found out that the broadcast had been a joke, she was angry enough to write a letter to *The Mercury Theatre*: "I do know that I am purely disgusted. Disrespectfully Yours."

In Lake Charles, Louisiana, the news bulletins from New York City worried Theodore and his family, who had relatives in the city. Gas fumes had killed thousands. People were falling into the East River. When the announcer on the roof of the Broadcasting Building collapsed from the poisonous black smoke, Theodore's eight-year-old son complained of "electricity in his stomach." Not until the final minutes of the show did the family discover that it had been a story. In Theodore's words, they were all "very much irritated by the harrowing experience."

In New York City, John called in his sons, nine and twelve, when the Princeton University astronomy professor began discussing Mars. Then the educational program transformed into a national emergency. The children panicked. John had no radio schedule to check. It took a while, though eventually the show "betrayed itself." They had been deceived, and John was unhappy about it. He wrote to CBS that night: "I . . . do not applaud but violently condemn what you have done."

IN THE DARK

Even as the program ended, others remained unaware that it had been a Mischief Night trick.

In the small town of Concrete, Washington, the power went out in the middle of the broadcast. Believing the outage was evidence of the Martian invasion, some townspeople packed up their families to escape into the mountains. The Earth had been saved by bacteria, but Concrete's residents didn't hear the good news.

At 9:30 Sunday night, Thomas R. was at a gas station near Warrenton, Virginia, when a car drove up behind him at the pump. The driver hopped out. Have you heard the dreadful reports? he asked. Thomas replied that he hadn't. The distressed man explained that "Mars had cracked open and great tanks of steel had fallen in New Jersey and great monsters had arisen." The Army had failed to fight them, and thousands were already dead. The government is telling everyone to evacuate the cities, the man said, and he was taking his family south. Thomas knew enough about science to realize that a Martian invasion couldn't be true. But the man was convinced.

Two Princeton University geology professors received word that a meteor had fallen just a few miles away from campus. Eager to investigate, they collected their equipment and drove out to the site. They were surprised to find that, not only was there no meteorite, but several other people were searching for it in the same spot. Later in the evening, the two men learned about the radio program and finally understood the source of the rumor.

The phones at the police department in Trenton, New Jersey, started ringing when the Martians began their annihilation. For two hours—even after the program ended—the department was inundated with about two thousand calls. According to the city manager, police operations were "crippled" and "paralyzed."

Some callers wanted to know if the radio reports were true. Others assumed they were and asked how many had died. Were there fires and gas attacks? Had the militia reported for duty? Relatives in other states called to check if family members had been killed. The police patiently informed them all that any rumors were due to a radio play.

The New Jersey State Police sent a squad of troopers with gas masks to Grovers Mill. They found only "would-be rescuers and thrill-seekers" crowding the local roads. The troopers' biggest challenge was calming people down and explaining that no meteors or Martians had fallen.

CITY OF TRENTON
NEW JERSEY

PAUL MORTON
CITY MANAGER
M. AM. SOC. C.E.

RECEIVED
NOV 15 1938

RAYMOND F. RICHTER
EXECUTIVE SECRETARY
AND
PERSONNEL OFFICER

October 31, 1938

44-3 WAR OF THE WORLDS

Federal Communications Commission
Washington, D. C.

COMPLAINT - WABC BROADCAST

Gentlemen:

To avoid a reoccurrence of a very grave and serious
situation that developed in this community last night,
due to the public's misinterpretation of the broadcast
through WABC at about 8:15, dramatizing H. G. Wells'
"War of the Worlds", which completely crippled communication facilities of our Police Department for
about three hours, I am requesting that you immediately make an investigation and do everything possible
to prevent a reoccurrence.

The situation was so acute that two thousand phone
calls were received in about two hours, all communication lines were paralyzed and voided normal municipal
functions. If we had had a large fire at this time it
could have easily caused a more serious situation.
Tremendous excitement existed among certain areas of
this community and we were receiving constantly long
distance phone calls from many states making inquiries
of relatives and families thought to have been killed
by the catastrophe that was included in the play.

I can conceive of no reason why the name of Trenton
and vicinity should have been used on this broadcast.
The State Police were equally handicapped and it is
indescribable the seriousness of this situation.

Your prompt attention will be appreciated.

Very truly yours,

PAUL MORTON
CITY MANAGER

PM/mlw

FILED IN
DEC 17 1938
D. M. & F. SEC.

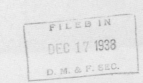

The day after the broadcast, the city manager of Trenton, New Jersey, sent this letter of complaint to the Federal Communications Commission (FCC). He explained that the radio program "completely crippled communication" at the police department for three hours, creating a serious situation.

MASS MURDERERS

Howard Koch listened to the show in his apartment. At nine o'clock, he turned off his radio and went to bed. He hadn't had much sleep all week, and soon he "was dead to the world." Koch never heard his phone ring. Houseman was trying to alert him to what was happening at CBS headquarters.

During the second part of the broadcast, police officers appeared at the control booth, wanting to know what was going on. They'd had reports of hysterical citizens on the streets.

As soon as Welles spoke his last word and removed his headphones, a CBS staffer told him he had a call in the control booth. A mayor in the Midwest was furious. His city's streets were full of people—some scared to death, others looting stores.

One public official yelled at Houseman over the phone, "If this is a joke we are coming down and punch you in the nose."

By then, several CBS executives had arrived at headquarters. They sent staff members into Studio One to confiscate all scripts of the radio play. Welles and Houseman were ushered into a back room for a half hour. Then CBS officials allowed in the reporters who had been clamoring to interview the two men.

Do you know how many have died because of your show? reporters asked. Have you heard about the suicides?

How could they answer questions like that? "Nobody was more surprised than we were," Houseman said later. "We believed for the next two or three hours that we were mass murderers."

CBS continued making on-air announcements until midnight, assuring listeners that there had not been a Martian invasion and that the program was "entirely fictitious." But according to the network, their telephone switchboards stayed "jammed with indignant listeners, some of them threatening to sue."

The New York headquarters of NBC, CBS's main competitor, received about six hundred phone calls asking if the invasion was real. At 9:30 p.m., NBC's news commentator Walter Winchell announced on his show that the attack hadn't actually happened.

WHAT HAD THEY DONE?!

Finally, CBS officials helped Welles and Houseman escape out a back door so that the press couldn't follow. The two men made their way several blocks to the Mercury's theatre. *Danton's Death* was opening in less than forty-eight hours, and they had a late-night rehearsal scheduled.

The streets of New York looked normal to them. No vehicles speeding wildly. No crowds of hysterical, suicidal people running down the sidewalks.

It was midnight when they arrived at the theatre. The cast was waiting.

"I don't know what's gonna happen. The police are gonna be after me," a shaken Welles told the actors. Amazed at the reaction to the broadcast, he exclaimed, "How are people so silly as to believe the thing like that[!]"

On the night of October 30, a photographer followed Welles and Houseman from CBS headquarters to their theatre rehearsal. As Welles stood in front of the curtain speaking to his cast, the photographer took this shot. The next morning, it appeared on newspaper front pages nationwide.

CHAPTER ELEVEN

EXTRA! EXTRA! READ ALL ABOUT IT!

"Radio Drama Terrorizes Thousands"

—Ogdensburg Journal, *October 31, 1938*

On Halloween morning, while Welles and Houseman were worrying about their futures in radio, Howard Koch got his first hint about the previous night's chaos. Walking from his Manhattan apartment to get a haircut, he picked up bits of conversation as people passed by. "Invasion." "Panic." Had the war in Europe started? he wondered.

His barber broke the news. "Haven't you heard?" He showed Koch a newspaper.

A bold headline ran across the front page: "Nation in Panic from Martian Radio Broadcast." Underneath was a photograph of a perplexed Orson Welles.

A declaration of war would have been less surprising to Koch. "Men, women and children . . . ," he later wrote, "were in flight from objects that had no existence except in their imaginations."

That Monday morning, the world awoke to news about "the wave of mass hysteria that swept the United States from coast to coast."

Front page headlines shouted: "Monsters of Mars on a Meteor Stampede Radiotic America"; "Hoax Spreads Terror Here; Some Pack Up. Roads Jammed—Fear Sends Several Persons to Hospitals"; "Radio Listeners in Panic, Taking War Drama as Fact"; "Many Fear World Coming to End."

Headlines like this one from Ogdensburg, New York, screamed the news.

EXCLUSIVE

Holding exclusive membership in The Associated Press in St. Lawrence County, The Journal each day offers its readers full coverage of world wide events.

Republican Established 1830
Journal Established 1855

Ogdensburg Journal

OGDENSBURG, N. Y., MONDAY, OCTOBER 31, 1938

THE WEATHER

Clear tonight. Tuesday fair, with rising temperature.

PRICE THREE CENTS

RADIO DRAMA TERRORIZES THOUSANDS

HORRIFYING!

According to the articles under the headlines, thousands of Americans thought that Martians had invaded.

New Jersey motorists, learning about the invasion on their car radios, headed west, "disregarding speed laws and curves in their race to escape the death rays." In Newark, hundreds fled, carrying as many possessions as they could. More than twenty families from one city block raced outside with faces covered to protect themselves from the gas attack.

In New York City, frantic people rushed into police stations asking where they should go for the evacuation. Their families, they said, were already loaded in the car. "Hundreds" of residents of Riverside Drive, on the west side of Manhattan, believed themselves to be in the path of the imaginary Martian tripods. Running into the street, they hurried toward Broadway. They didn't stop until a cab driver, who had been listening to the radio broadcast, told them it was just a play.

Articles claimed that "at least a score" of people needed medical care for hysteria and shock, and that "many were injured in the widespread panic" as they tried to flee. Newspapers across the country carried a photograph of a woman with her left arm in a sling and her knees bandaged. The woman, a New York City actress, was described as a "casualty" and "victim" of the Martian broadcast. The caption explained that she fell down stairs in her rush to escape when she heard that the poisonous smoke had reached Times Square.

The Halloween headline from the *New York Telegram*

Newspapers reported that hundreds of nurses and doctors called the Newark police to volunteer their help with the injured. Trenton police received

U. S. Investigates Radio Drama of Invasion By Martians That Threw Nation Into Panic

desperate requests for the poison gas antidote. A man phoned his local police station in the Bronx, a New York City borough, certain the invaders were bombing New Jersey because he saw the smoke from his roof.

PANIC FAR AND WIDE

The panic occurred outside New York and New Jersey, too. A man from Dayton, Ohio, called the *New York Times* asking, "What time will it be the end of the world?" A Pittsburgh man came home to find his screaming wife about to swallow poison. She said she wanted to die that way rather than be killed by the Martians.

The *Los Angeles Times* received hundreds of calls during and immediately after the radio program. Saying they had relatives in the New Jersey–New York area, people wanted to know if lists of casualties were available.

In Providence, residents phoned the electric company, asking it to switch off the lights "so that the city would be safe from the enemy."

Even the foreign press carried the story. In Germany, newspapers printed articles about America's "war scare." Headlines read: "Death Ray Panic in New York—Half of America Flees to Bomb Proof Cellars" and "American People in Uproar—Radio Causes Mass Panic—Indescribable Results of War Agitation." Reports claimed that Adolf Hitler commented on the Martian panic in a speech.

Similar headlines and articles continued into Tuesday, November 1. By then, many newspapers had published the program's script, which CBS released to the press. Before the extensive newspaper coverage ended, it reached far more people than those who heard the broadcast on Mischief Night.

SENSATIONAL

Many of the headlines and articles contained dramatic language and exaggeration. The *New York Journal and American* stated: "MILLIONS OF PEOPLE understood the broadcast to be REAL." The *New-York World Telegram* described the reaction to the broadcast as an "epidemic of fear that has no parallel in our history." The press had good reason to play up the event. Sensational stories sell newspapers.

Some journalists may have had an additional motive. Newspapers and radio had been competing for audience and advertisers ever since radio's popularity began growing. Numerous articles and editorials declared that the *Mercury* broadcast was an illustration of why radio was less trustworthy as a news source than the printed press.

Although newspapers had embellished incidents and inflated the numbers of panicked people, their stories weren't totally wrong. CBS and *The Mercury Theatre* received telegrams, phone calls, and letters that supported some of those accounts.

Listeners reported that they or a person they knew had experienced a heart attack, shortness of breath, or a nervous breakdown. The victims had to call a doctor and take medicine to calm down or sleep. According to one nurse in Connecticut, a woman

On the morning after the broadcast, the news media swept into Grovers Mill, New Jersey, looking for a story. Photographers convinced local people to pose. In this photo, area resident William Dock pretends to defend himself from the Martians.

she was caring for "suffered a heart attack, while one of her little boys became hysterical and another began to vomit."

People wrote that they had rushed to be with loved ones or tried to escape when they heard that the invaders were on the move.

Although the mention of "Martians" tipped off many listeners, not everyone heard that word. Some jumped to the conclusion that the invaders were German Nazis. One person later admitted, "When the announcer kept calling them people from Mars I just thought he was ignorant and didn't know yet that Hitler had sent them all."

Others joined *The Mercury Theatre* late and assumed the worst. At 8:00 p.m. Eastern Time, millions of Americans were listening to the top-rated *Chase and Sanborn Hour* on NBC. About fifteen minutes into the show, popular ventriloquist Edgar Bergen and his wooden dummy Charlie McCarthy finished their comedy skit. When a singer came on next, uninterested listeners twirled their dial to find an alternative . . . and tuned to *The Mercury Theatre* just as the Martian emerged from the cylinder. Mesmerized by the astonishing news on CBS, they didn't go back to Charlie McCarthy.

"DEEPLY REGRETFUL"

CBS president William Paley and other nervous executives were quite displeased with Welles, Houseman, and the Mercury. The network was worried it might face lawsuits and new government regulations because of the panic.

H. G. Wells's literary agent told the press that he never authorized changes to the original story that could cause such alarm. He and Wells were "deeply concerned" and wanted a retraction from CBS and Orson Welles.

Going into damage control, CBS announced its regret that a few listeners who had heard only parts of the program "mistook fantasy for fact." The network emphasized that four statements described the program as a drama—at the beginning, on either side of the station break, and at the end. To avoid future misunderstandings, however, CBS programs would no longer use "a simulated news broadcast within a dramatization" that could confuse listeners.

The National Association of Broadcasters shared CBS's concerns about government control of radio. The organization expressed regret that the program upset people. Its president said that the group was determined "to fulfill to the highest degree our obligation to the public."

On Halloween afternoon, October 31, CBS arranged for Orson Welles to meet the press and answer questions. The future of the network, *The Mercury Theatre on the Air*, and Welles's career rested on how he handled himself.

Unshaven and cradling his pipe in his right hand, Welles took his seat in front of flash and newsreel cameras. He was surrounded by a couple dozen reporters, notepads and pencils ready to write down everything he said. The broadcast and its aftermath had become the week's leading story. Clips of the press conference would later appear as part of short newsreels shown before movies in theaters nationwide.

With furrowed brow, Welles explained that since the broadcast, he hadn't read the newspapers or slept much. In a prepared statement, he said, "Of course, we are deeply shocked and deeply regretful about the results of last night's broadcast." He expressed bewilderment that anyone believed the broadcast was a real news event. After all, the program had been aired at the regular *Mercury Theatre* time and was listed in radio schedules.

"It came rather as a great surprise to us that a story . . . ," Welles gazed directly into the newsreel camera, "the original for so many succeeding comic strips and adventure stories and novels about a mythical invasion by monsters from the planet Mars, should have had so profound an effect upon radio listeners."

Welles told reporters that the *Mercury* team had almost not chosen to perform *The War of the Worlds* because they thought "people might be bored or annoyed at hearing a tale so improbable."

A reporter asked if Welles had taken advantage of his audience by pretending to use "authentic news." Welles responded that this method didn't originate with *The Mercury Theatre* and was, in fact, used by other radio programs. "It would seem to me unlikely that . . . an invasion from Mars would find ready acceptance," he said. "I was frankly terribly shocked to learn that it did."

On October 31, Orson Welles met with reporters, answering their questions and expressing his bewilderment over the public's reaction to his show.

Another reporter inquired whether there should be a law against similar radio dramatizations. Welles replied that he didn't "know what the legislation would be. . . . Radio is new," he continued, "and we are learning about the effect it has on people. We've learned a terrible lesson."

Despite Welles's apologetic words, some observers questioned his sincerity. They noted that, as a talented actor, he had performed his part flawlessly.

Sincere or not, would Welles's performance save his radio program . . . and his career?

DEAR MR. WELLES

No one knows the total number of letters and telegrams sent to CBS, *The Mercury Theatre on the Air*, or Orson Welles, beginning on the night of the broadcast. One 1940 report claimed that nearly 1,800 people wrote to CBS, of which 60 percent were positive. This correspondence has been lost, however. About 1,400 letters sent to Welles and *The Mercury Theatre* survive in library archives. Less than 10 percent criticize Welles and the broadcast. Here are excerpts.

"I listened to your radio play Sunday night and it was a humdinger."
D. R., Davenport, Iowa

"Personally, I'd rather you'd soap my windows, or throw corn on the porch—the same porch that I thought (to hear you) wouldn't be here very long." *M. K., Mitchell, Indiana*

"The American public got a slight taste of the fear which overshadows the people of Europe constantly." *J. S., Phoenix, Arizona*

"I have been chosen as [representative] to tell you how sorry we all are that the people didn't like your play. . . . What ever happens because of your radio play you will know that a dozen children will stick by you." *N. C., Chicago, Illinois*

"I sincerely hope this broadcast won't affect future ones as I look forward to them each week." *M. N., Little Rock, Arkansas*

"Mr. Hitler must be laughing his head off (if he ever laughs) to think what cowards we are."
Mrs. G. T., Maplewood, New Jersey

"It is a good thing that we have strong hearts otherwise we would have been dead from fright. . . . We hate to admit it— but the acting was simply superb."
H. L. S. and A. W. H., Denver, Colorado

"Despite the fact that the neighborhood as a whole is instituting a mass movement to string you to a tree, rest assured that you have a few faithful backers. . . . Perhaps the nation needs to be embarrassed by its own ignorance once in a while."
M. H., Bronx, New York

"Aren't you ashamed of yourself—well I'll not tell you what I am thinking because you would probely [*sic*] have me arrested."
E. B., Marion, Indiana

"Orchids to you and razzberries to those presumably intelligent Americans who can't take a joke when it's on themselves. . . . Yours until the Martians come."
R. W., Takoma Park, Maryland

"We trust that the air was released from your auto tires and your windows thoroughly soaped."
Mr. and Mrs. F. H., Albuquerque, New Mexico

"If what I think of you would ever take effect it would burn you up to a cinder. Hopeing [*sic*] never to hear from you again." *M. Z., Dover, New Jersey*

"These mollicoddled jitterbugs show what they're made of. Just a bunch of <u>cry babies</u>."
Mrs. S. S., Dearborn, Michigan

"Perhaps if you'd put on your little play fifty years ago it would have been a joke but the way science has progressed in that time, surely nothing is impossible. . . . Scorchingly . . ."
M. M., Oklahoma City, Oklahoma

"I think the safest place for you is Mars. Take a rocket and get going. . . . Nuts to you!"
G. H., San Francisco, California

"There was only one thing wrong about the location. Why didn't you set it in Berlin and destroy Mr. Hitler?"
Miss D. H., Paterson, New Jersey

"Don't people THINK anymore? My God, what the propagandists of the next war can do!!"
E. C., Hartford, Connecticut

"You have made radio a medium of deception which if allowed to continue could make radio a menace."
M. J., Elmwood Park, Illinois

"It shakes one's faith in democracy to think that such hysteria and panic can affect people who are supposed to vote intelligently next week."
D. O'G., Notre Dame, Indiana

"The infernal machines passed within a few blocks from my house . . . and I didn't think to step outside to see them. After New York was destroyed we all went to bed." *P. V. W., Elizabeth, New Jersey*

"All this goes to illustrate the low mentality of the average listener. They do not see 1/10 of what they read. They must not listen to 1/2 of what they hear."
R. I., East Cleveland, Ohio

CHAPTER TWELVE

FALLOUT

> "This only goes to prove . . . that the intelligent people were all listening to a dummy, and all the dummies were listening to you."
>
> —*Telegram to Orson Welles*

No sooner had the Sunday night broadcast ended than the demands for government action began. Iowa senator Clyde Herring announced that he planned to introduce a bill in the U.S. Congress to control "such abuses." "Radio has no more right to present programs like that," said Herring, "than someone has in knocking on your door and screaming."

The senator wasn't the only one concerned about the broadcasters' judgment. The Federal Communications Commission (FCC), established by the Communications Act of 1934, oversaw radio broadcasting and issued its licenses. The FCC chairman, Frank McNinch, announced Monday morning that his agency would investigate. "Any broadcast that creates such general panic and fear …," he stated, "is, to say the least, regrettable."

FCC chairman Frank McNinch (1873–1950) testifying at a U.S. Senate committee hearing in January 1939

FCC commissioner
T. A. M. Craven
(1893–1972)

But one of his fellow seven commissioners, T. A. M. Craven, noted that the FCC should be cautious about censorship. "The public," he said, "does not want a 'spineless' radio."

IN OUR OPINION . . .

On Tuesday, November 1, newspaper editorial pages started reacting to the broadcast.

The *New York World-Telegram* declared: "We don't agree with those who are arguing that the Sunday night scare shows a need for strict government censorship of radio programs. On the contrary, we think it is evidence of how dangerous political control of radio might become. If so many people could be misled unintentionally, when the purpose was merely to entertain, what could designing politicians not do through control of broadcasting stations."

An opinion column in the *Boston Daily Globe* said that the Welles broadcast revealed a fact many Americans didn't understand: Radio has the potential "for spreading alarm to the unthinking or ill-informed." To resist propaganda, the columnist continued, people need to apply "a healthy skepticism" to what they read and hear.

Influential opinion writer Dorothy Thompson did not mince words. In her newspaper column, which appeared nationwide on Wednesday, November 2, she wrote that Orson Welles had "shown up the incredible stupidity, lack of nerve[,] and ignorance of thousands." The *Mercury Theatre* team deserved a medal for shining a warning light on the way European dictators like Hitler, Mussolini, and Stalin used radio to "incite hatreds, inflame masses, . . . abolish reason and maintain themselves in power."

American journalist and radio news commentator Dorothy Thompson (1893–1961) in 1939. Thompson was known for her criticism of Adolf Hitler, and she was expelled from Nazi Germany in 1934 because of her reporting.

ARX
OMNIVM
NATIONVM

Italian dictator Benito Mussolini
(1883–1945) addressing a crowd.
Mussolini, allied with Germany, led
Italy into World War II.

Editorial writer Heywood Broun also connected the panic to the crisis in Europe. "The course of world history has affected national psychology. Jitters have come to roost."

The *London Times* of Great Britain pointed out the folly of the United States in the face of serious international threats. "Here is a nation which, alone of big nations, has deemed it unnecessary to rehearse for protection against attack from the air by fellow-beings on this earth and suddenly believes itself—and for little enough reason—faced with a more fearful attack from another world."

The *Washington Post*, however, criticized the broadcast. "So long as radio serves as an organ for the broadcasting of information as well as entertainment it ought to keep a clear line of distinction between the two functions."

The *New York Times* also disapproved of mixing news and fiction. "What began as 'entertainment'," the editorial said, "might readily have ended in disaster." The newspaper called on broadcasters to regulate themselves. "Radio is new but it has adult responsibilities."

IRATE

People who had been duped by the broadcast were angry at Welles and CBS. So were many who read newspaper accounts of the panic, even though they hadn't heard the broadcast themselves. Starting the night of the show, they let the federal authorities know it.

Most addressed their letters, postcards, and telegrams to FCC chairman McNinch, whose name appeared in newspapers the day after the broadcast. A handful wrote to the Federal Radio Commission (which had been replaced by the FCC in 1934), President Roosevelt, the "Secretary of the Interior" (few knew that his name was Harold L. Ickes), or the FBI. All letters were forwarded to the FCC.

Comments included protests that, despite what CBS claimed, there had NOT been four announcements to inform listeners that the broadcast was a radio drama. (In fact, there were.) And why wasn't the station break at half past the hour as everyone expected during entertainment programs?

Several letter writers complained that Orson Welles and his cohorts intentionally misled the public by naming actual towns, roads, and government agencies. One North Carolina woman wrote: "Who was I to question Princeton scientist the War [Department] at Washington the Red Cross and other names for which we have the greatest respect and reverance [sic]. I thot [sic] there must be something to it."

Letters called for the FCC to remove Welles and CBS from the air, fine them, or assume control of *all* radio broadcasts because the networks had shown themselves to be irresponsible.

A man from New Jersey wrote that fake news undermines "the prestige of the radio as a dispenser of news." Other people agreed that the trustworthiness of radio had been damaged. It was a principal source of information, especially if the nation

was ever attacked by an enemy. They had believed radio news more than newspapers. CBS, especially, had earned a reputation for reliability thanks to its reports on the European conflict. On October 30, radio—and CBS—deceived the public.

The president of the Association of Radio News Editors and Writers weighed in with a telegram to the FCC: "'News Bulletin' and 'Flash'…when misplaced tend to confuse the listener and lessen his attention when true news is delivered. . . . [It] is detrimental to newscasting and dangerous."

DON'T CENSOR!

During the five weeks after the broadcast, the FCC received more than six hundred letters, postcards, and telegrams. Although the majority criticized Welles and his program, others urged against government action as punishment.

One New Yorker told the FCC: "The freedom of the press and the radio is and should remain of vital interest to all of us, regardless of our political or religious beliefs, since freedom once lost is very difficult to win back."

Some editorial writers pointed out that gullible Americans were susceptible to propaganda such as the kind used in Germany. A poster from about 1934 encourages German students to spread the principles of Nazism on behalf of Führer Adolf Hitler.

A high-school English teacher from Iowa wrote: "It isn't his [Orson Welles's] fault that people are so '*dumb.*' . . . Please don't do as Senator Herring wants—all programs tuned to the intelligence of a child."

People wrote to newspapers and magazines with similar views. In a letter to the editor of his local newspaper, one Connecticut man said that he was opposed to the government telling "radio stations what they can or cannot broadcast—in a supposedly free country!" He suggested that the FCC stay out of it and that Senator Herring instead work on "providing jobs for some 12 millions of people!"

A *Time* magazine reader from Ohio wrote to its editor: "Leave the listening public the right to dial to its own level of intelligence."

Senator Clyde Herring of Iowa (1879–1945) pushed for a federal law allowing the FCC to review radio programs before they aired. No law was passed.

CAN'T FOOL ME

The FCC also heard from those who had not been tricked and were surprised that anyone could be so gullible. Letter writers explained that they recognized the H. G. Wells story and Orson Welles's voice as Professor Pierson. Others caught the program's introduction or saw *The War of the Worlds* listed in their newspapers' radio schedules.

Some listeners missed the program's beginning and, at first, believed the newsflashes. But they realized the truth long before the station break. A few switched to another station to check. Others found out—from a friend, family member, police officer, or newspaper office—that they were tuned to a radio drama.

Several people who wrote letters recounted how they sniffed out the hoax. A thirteen-year-old Minnesota girl said that she knew "by studying the Solar System in school, if any such thing would happen scientists would know about one year before the incident."

An Alabama woman thought everybody should realize that an attack from Mars was "not only highly improbable, . . . but an absolute impossibility at present."

Who could believe that such creatures existed? commented a Utah man.

A North Carolina listener wasn't fooled for a minute. If Martians attacked and carried out that much destruction, she reasoned, they'd create "so much static that a radio program could not even be heard."

Others picked up on the rapid travel of Carl Phillips from Princeton to Grovers Mill. One New Yorker noted "that the entire land forces of the American army in the East [was] mobilized in a few seconds," New Jersey conquered, and the population of New York City either evacuated or annihilated "within a few minutes."

These and other letter writers considered the program simply enjoyable entertainment. High-school students from Tulsa, Oklahoma, sent the FCC a petition with sixty-six signatures asking that CBS air *The War of the Worlds* again. Despite pleas from fans and those who missed the show, CBS did not repeat it.

THE VERDICT

In early December, Chairman McNinch announced that the FCC was dismissing all complaints it had received about the October 30 broadcast. The Communications Act of 1934 did not give the commission the authority to censor programs, he said. Furthermore, CBS had not violated any regulations. The FCC was satisfied that the network had taken steps "sufficient to protect the public interest" in the future.

The U.S. Congress did not pass Senator Herring's bill or any others that would censor radio programs.

Orson Welles, the Mercury, and CBS faced thousands of dollars worth of lawsuits for personal injury, mental anguish, and damages. In one of the smaller claims, an Illinois man complained that his frightened wife had a nervous breakdown and was incapacitated for a month. He demanded $60, the amount she would have earned as a dressmaker's assistant had she been able to work, plus $18 for medical care.

A man from Virginia wrote: "I wasted exactly $3.37 [for a ticket to escape] on which I was going to buy an Arrow Shirt and a tie. . . . So if you would be so kind you could send me a shirt (16–4 <u>size</u>) and tie."

Fortunately for Welles and Houseman, their lawyer had added a clause to their CBS contract ensuring that they and the Mercury would not be liable for their show's content.

Despite the legal threats, none of the lawsuits made it to court. No evidence emerged that anyone had been injured or died—suicide or otherwise—as a result of the broadcast. The story about the woman who broke her arm was discredited because the victim was an actress eager to get her photograph in the newspapers. A family in Baltimore claimed that their sixty-year-old father suffered a heart attack after becoming excited during the broadcast and died two weeks later. There was no proof that the program had caused his attack.

At the end of the year, newspaper editors and press groups listed the Martian broadcast among 1938's biggest news stories. *That* was saying something in light of Hitler's rise in Europe, the Nazi persecution of Jews, the New England hurricane, the business and employment slump, and the war between China and Japan.

Orson Welles was even nominated as *Time* magazine's Man of the Year for 1938. He deserved the honor, one reader said, because he "taught us a lesson" about the real danger of a sudden attack on the country by foreign dictators.

The magazine's editors chose Adolf Hitler instead.

Telegram to the Federal Radio Commission from the legal department of Newark, New Jersey, protesting the *War of the Worlds* broadcast. The date stamps indicate when the telegram was received in Washington and sent to the appropriate office.

Received at 708 14th St., N. W. Washington, D. C.

PA14 46 6 EXTRA NL=NEWARK NJ 30

FEDERAL RADIO COMMISSION=

WASHDC=

AS VICTIM OF EFFECT OF PROGRAM QUOTE THE WAR OF WORLDS BROADCAST OVER COLUMBIA BROADCASTING SYSTEM BY H B WELLS ENTER MY PROTEST DEMAND DRASTIC ACTION BE TAKEN AGAINST BROADCASTING COMPANY HEALTH AND LIFE OF NEWARK CITIZENS SHOULD BE CONSIDERED=

WILLIAM S CANTALUPO   ASSISTANT CORPORATION COUNSEL

CITY OF NEWARK.

DEAR FCC

The Federal Communications Commission received more than six hundred letters and telegrams about the *War of the Worlds* radio broadcast. About 60 percent of them criticized Welles and his program. Here are samples of both pro and con opinions.

"If some action is not taken, the citizens of this country will have to agitate for complete control of all radio broadcasting by the Federal Government." *J. H., New York, New York*

"I was one of the thousands who heard this program and did <u>not</u> jump out of the window, did <u>not</u> attempt suicide, did <u>not</u> break my arm while beating a hasty retreat from my apartment, did <u>not</u> anticipate a horrible death." *J. Y., Aberdeen, South Dakota*

"It may be well to consider . . . that should a real emergency arise and should a warning be broadcast; would the people heed that warning or having been fooled once before, turn their radios off with a remark 'another radio drama.'" *T. B., New York, New York*

"They performed a great public service in showing the people who did become frightened that they should not be so gullible." *J. C., Butte, Montana*

"I am annoyed by Radio's willingness to let this country be the laughing stock of Europe—at a time when national prestige is no joke—rather than admit its hoax." *L. M., Sanbornton, New Hampshire*

"We knew it was a story, and I wasn't scared at all." *M. J., age eleven, Rockford, Illinois*

"Having just experienced a Hurricane and flood we were in no condition to listen to such a program."
Mrs. G. N., Springfield, Vermont

"If a petition against such broadcasts would help in any way, I, for one, can guarantee at least 50 names of responsible persons who would be willing and eager to protest."
D. H., Brooklyn, New York

"If one has read at all, even the local daily papers (which is the least one could read) one would know we are not receiving messages from Mars at this present date."
L. D., Royal Oak, Michigan

"I wouldn't permit my family to turn on W.A.B.C. again if it were the only station to broadcast. . . . I only hope that the author of pain suffers as he has made thousands suffer. I am so incensed I can't even write."
R. F., Ridgefield Park, New Jersey

"Perhaps you could educate people who are inclined to be nervous, to the fact that the little button that controls the dial will at a touch immediately tune out any programs they do not wish to hear."
Mrs. M. P., Washington State

"I have one little girl who is very nervous and she kept saying . . . 'I don't want to die.' . . . If such programs continue I will make kindling wood of my receiving set."
T. S., Clarksburg, West Virginia

"Dont [sic] you think instead of investigating that we should hang our heads in shame to know that such a great number of the citizens of these United States have the Mentality and emotional stability of an EIGHT Year Old.
E. C., Charlotte, North Carolina

"The citizens of this Country demand that this crowd be punished."

J. S., Americus, Georgia

"My wife and sister-in-law have heart trouble and I'll assure you had this horrifying program been fatal to either of them the Columbia Company would have had to answer for it."

A. P., Baltimore, Maryland

"The trouble with us in this country we are not war concious [sic] and we have laughed off any chances of foreign powers attacking us." J. J., Mason, Michigan

"CBS program of last evening most abominable hoax ever perpetrated on American public."

J. S., Tylertown, Mississippi

"Those who were upset by that broadcast represent that small minority whose dullness prevents their distinguishing fantasy and reality. . . . There may be a solid argument for their institutionalization."

Dr. A. C., Indianapolis, Indiana

"We need a radio dictator, just as the movies, baseball have."

L. H., Burns, Oregon

"Be assured that McCarthy [NBC's popular dummy] would not be mowin' 'em down while a group of Martians marched toward Radio City."

L. S., Nashville, Tennessee

CHAPTER THIRTEEN

"TOO DARN REALISTIC"

"It was only a ventriloquist and his dummy that prevented a panic from developing into a major catastrophe."

—*Letter to the* New York Post

Why did a fictional Martian invasion scare so many people?

Orson Welles had his own theory, which he shared in a 1940 *Saturday Evening Post* interview. He thought that the previous two generations had been coddled too much because of "mistaken theories of education." In his view, "the ban on gruesome fairy tales, terrifying nursemaids and other standard sources of horror, has left most of the population" vulnerable to scary stories and situations.

HOW MANY PANICKED?

Scientists who studied psychology and the effects of radio were interested in the public's reaction to the broadcast, too. Immediately after news of the panic broke, a group of Princeton University researchers set out to understand what happened. Headed by Hadley Cantril, the Princeton Radio Research Project conducted a study of those who had been spooked.

Using surveys from two polling companies, the researchers calculated that 6 million people across the United States heard the *Mercury Theatre* broadcast. They estimated that between 1.5 million and 2 million of these listeners believed they were hearing actual news. More than 1 million of them became rattled by it.

To learn more, the researchers interviewed 135 people within a month of the broadcast, all from New Jersey. Of this group, 107 were chosen because they admitted being frightened.

When the study was published in 1940, the authors acknowledged that the interview group was not a "proper sample of the total population." They claimed that their results were reliable anyway. Critics of the study point to the selection process as a major flaw.

Why did these listeners think that New Jersey had been invaded and their own lives threatened? According to the researchers, the *Mercury* had produced a broadcast that was *too* realistic. The entertainers duped people by interrupting a musical program with newsflashes, which the public had come to trust. Listeners were convinced when they heard familiar names of roads and towns, as well as comments by experts and officials.

The Princeton study concluded that many who became afraid tuned in after the program's introduction identified it as a drama. Others had their radio on in the background and weren't paying close attention at first.

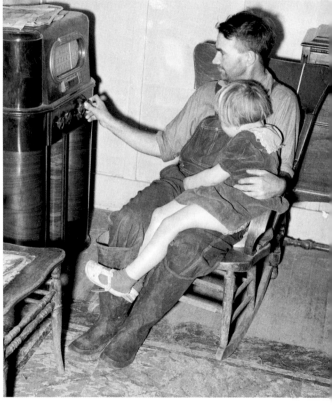

Some people were initially fooled but eventually figured out that the program wasn't real. Listeners who continued to believe were the most likely to panic, even running away or hiding. One frightened person didn't check other stations to verify the news because, she explained, the announcers said CBS "was the only one not destroyed."

THE MYTH

The *War of the Worlds* broadcast was based on fake news. In a twist, the story of a widespread panic wasn't true either.

For decades, the Princeton study was cited as evidence that the Halloween broadcast caused mass hysteria. But by today's standards, the 1938 surveys and interviews were not conducted scientifically. The polling samples were biased toward those who thought the broadcast was real, and the statistical analyses of the data were flawed.

In truth, no one knows how many people heard the broadcast from the beginning and how many switched to it partway through. There is no accurate count of how many listeners believed it and how many became terrified.

A man and his daughter enjoy a radio program. On the night of October 30, 1938, only a small percentage of the national radio audience was tuned to CBS's *War of the Worlds* broadcast.

The usual audience for *The Mercury Theatre on the Air* was about only a tenth of the thirty-five million people who tuned to *The Chase and Sanborn Hour*. The audience size on October 30 was, therefore, probably much smaller than the six million estimated by the Princeton study.

Letters to the FCC and Orson Welles confirm that people in all parts of the nation were alarmed by the broadcast. The most letters came from areas close to the "invasion" site in New Jersey and New York, where the perceived threat was greatest.

Yet few of the two thousand letters mention a person hysterical enough to escape the Martians by leaving his or her home. The number of Americans who panicked was likely far fewer than one million, the number claimed by the Princeton study.

GULLIBLE AMERICANS?

The extent of the panic was overstated by the press, too. More than twelve thousand articles were published about the broadcast during the three weeks after it aired, though the story was on the front pages just two or three days.

Incidents of people running for their lives or being treated for shock were repeated nearly word for word in newspapers across the country. This created the impression that the hysteria was more widespread than it really was.

In the newspapers' rush to get out the daily edition on deadline, most of these articles were printed before reporters verified them. Many stories turned out to be exaggerations. Traffic on roads and streets was not unusual that night, casting doubt on accounts of tens of thousands of people fleeing on foot or in their cars.

Phones at CBS in New York City were definitely overloaded. The police did receive a higher volume of calls, particularly near the imaginary landing site. But the New Jersey Bell Telephone Company later said that the number of calls placed that night had increased by just 6 or 7 percent. That was hardly the staggering amount reported in newspapers. Many of the calls to CBS and the police were from radio listeners trying to confirm what they'd heard, not reacting in panic.

The overwhelming majority of listeners recognized the broadcast as a radio play. Even among those agitated enough to write letters, only about a quarter said the program had scared them to any degree. A small number of those people admitted to panicking.

It's fair to say the broadcast fooled thousands of people, at least temporarily. But the press and the Princeton study painted a picture of nationwide mass hysteria. That led Americans to an inaccurate view of how their fellow citizens behaved. For eighty years, this false story has been repeated in textbooks, popular books, articles, and movies.

In reality, the United States wasn't as gullible as it had been portrayed.

FOOL ME TWICE, SHAME ON ME

Despite the international news coverage of the 1938 broadcast, later radio versions of *The War of the Worlds* deceived the public, too.

In November 1944, a station in Santiago, Chile, tried the broadcast again. Newsflashes declared that Martians had defeated the military and taken over its bases. The radio station and local newspapers advertised the fictional program during the previous week. Still, according to news reports after the broadcast, thousands of panicked Chileans hid in their houses or ran away.

A few years later, the response to a similar broadcast in Ecuador's capital was more extreme. On a Saturday night in February 1949, Radio Quito announced a Martian invasion using the newsflash technique and local place names. When some of the distressed listeners realized that they had been tricked, they formed an angry mob. The crowd set fire to the radio station, destroying it and the newspaper offices housed in the same building.

Police didn't arrive right away because they had gone to the supposed site of the Martian landing outside the city. Before the Ecuadorian army could bring calm using tanks and tear gas, several people were killed. The exact number varies from two to twenty, depending on the news source.

Mars Invasion Hoax Brings Death to 15

Angry Ecuador Mobs Burn Newspaper, Radio Station

QUITO, Eucador, Feb. 14 (P)—Fifteen persons were killed and at least 15 in...

Headline from the *Los Angeles Daily Mirror* about the *War of the Worlds* broadcast in Quito, Ecuador, on February 12, 1949

Thirty years after the original *Mercury* broadcast, it happened again in western New York State. On Halloween night 1968, radio station WKBW in Buffalo aired its own version, complete with sound effects. Using an outline updating the 1938 script, the station's deejay and news reporters ad-libbed eyewitness accounts of a Martian attack.

The station had advertised the Halloween special for three weeks, and the broadcast was interrupted with announcements that it was a dramatization. Yet many listeners believed that their favorite radio personalities had been killed and the Buffalo area taken over by extraterrestrials. The station was swamped with phone calls.

Today, Orson Welles and the talented *Mercury* team are given credit for producing an exceptional radio program. The reaction to these later broadcasts suggests there was more to the *Mercury*'s success: the H. G. Wells story itself. The man who crafted it more than one hundred years ago knew how to shake up an audience.

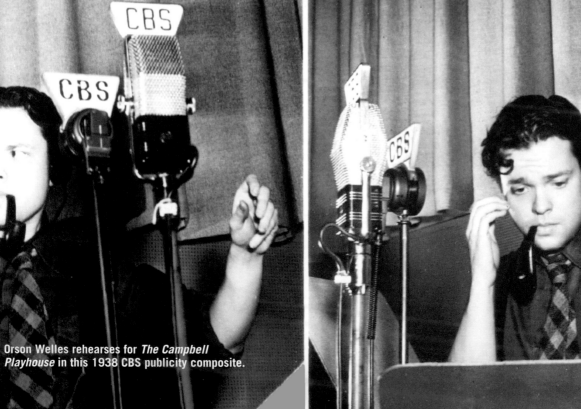

Orson Welles rehearses for *The Campbell Playhouse* in this 1938 CBS publicity composite.

CHAPTER FOURTEEN

SOFT LANDING

" Any man that could cause that kind
of upheaval in a whole country, from
coast-to-coast, has got to be great."

—*Switchboard operator on duty October 31, 1938*

Despite the tidal wave of reaction to the broadcast (or maybe because of it), CBS did not cancel *The Mercury Theatre on the Air*. In fact, within a week of the Martian invasion, the Campbell Soup Company offered to sponsor the series, moving it from Sunday to Friday evenings. On December 9, 1938, under the new name *The Campbell Playhouse*, the *Mercury* team presented a drama based on the novel *Rebecca*.

Unlike the original show, which had no breaks for advertising, it now included soup commercials. John Houseman later remarked: "I guess they figured if Orson could make the War of the Worlds credible and the Martians credible, he could make Campbell's Chicken Soup credible."

ORSON WELLES

The Halloween Eve broadcast turned Orson Welles into an international celebrity, and Hollywood came courting. In 1939, he headed to California to make movies. Welles produced, wrote, directed, and starred in several path-breaking films, including the 1941 classic *Citizen Kane*.

For that movie, he used actors who had played roles in the *War of the Worlds* broadcast and other Mercury radio and theatre productions. Bernard Herrmann, the *Mercury Theatre*'s orchestra leader, composed and conducted the musical score. In a nod to the Martian broadcast, the main character played by Welles, Charles Foster Kane, says early in the movie, "Don't believe everything you hear on the radio."

Citizen Kane was nominated for nine Academy Awards. Welles and writer Herman Mankiewicz shared the award for Best Original Screenplay. Herrmann earned a nomination for his score, and he went on to provide music for dozens of movies from the 1940s through the 1970s.

In October 1940, Welles met the author whose ingenious 1897 story had brought the actor stardom. H. G. Wells was visiting the United States on a speaking tour to encourage American support for Britain in the war against Germany. Both men happened to be in San Antonio, Texas, at the same time. A local radio station invited them to be interviewed on October 28, two days before the Martian broadcast's second anniversary.

Orson Welles and H. G. Wells meet in San Antonio, Texas, in October 1940. Here, they discuss the ongoing war in Europe.

Although Wells had complained earlier about the way his novel was altered for the *Mercury* broadcast, the resulting publicity increased sales of his books. He complimented Welles on-air, calling the 1938 radio program a "sensational Halloween spree." H. G. Wells died six years later in London, a few weeks before his eightieth birthday.

Years after the *War of the Worlds* broadcast, Orson Welles claimed that he always intended it to scare people. He said he wanted to teach them a lesson about trusting everything on the radio. But Welles was a notorious storyteller. In their memoirs, both John Houseman and Howard Koch denied his account. They wrote that Welles and the entire *Mercury* team had been completely surprised by the public's reaction.

Throughout his long career in the United States and Europe, Welles worked in stage, radio, film, and television. He was honored with several awards during his lifetime. Yet Welles created his most successful and well-known productions—the *War of the Worlds* broadcast and *Citizen Kane*—before he turned twenty-six. He died of a heart attack on October 10, 1985.

JOHN HOUSEMAN

In 1939, John Houseman joined Welles in Hollywood and helped edit the *Citizen Kane* script. Despite their close ties working together in New York, their relationship became rocky. During a dispute over the finances of the Mercury company in December 1939, an intoxicated Welles threw a serving dish and burning can of Sterno at Houseman. With that, Houseman dissolved their business partnership, which, he later wrote, "withered and died in the blast of [Welles's] sudden fame."

For the next five decades, Houseman edited and wrote screenplays, earning admiration for his work. A radio and film veteran called him "one of the greatest editors I've ever known." Houseman also

John Houseman at the National Film Society Convention in 1979

directed, produced, and acted in movies and television. Among his honors was the Academy Award for Best Supporting Actor for the 1973 film *The Paper Chase*. Besides his Hollywood work, he spent time in New York City, teaching drama and producing plays.

When Welles was asked about Houseman during an interview in 1963, twenty-five years after the Martian broadcast, he refused to talk about his former friend. "He's one of the few subjects," Welles replied, "that depresses me so deeply that it really spoils my day to think of him." Years later, Welles acknowledged that Houseman made possible the staging of the Mercury's theatre productions. "Without his gifts as a bureaucratic finagler, the shows just wouldn't have got on. I owe him much. Leave it at that."

Howard Koch once observed: "What happened to Orson's career is that he became a celebrity. That became his life and sapped his talent. And he lost John Houseman, and that was a very solid base for him to work from."

Geraldine Fitzgerald, a Mercury actress, agreed. "[Welles] needed . . . someone exactly like Houseman, and he didn't have that person . . . who could stand between him and the world, and work things out for him. He really did need that."

Houseman was generally complimentary in his comments about Welles. In 1948, he wrote that "'The War of the Worlds' was a magic act, one of the world's greatest, and Orson was just the man to bring it off."

John Houseman died of cancer on October 31, 1988, one day after the fiftieth anniversary of the famous broadcast.

HOWARD KOCH

Howard Koch continued writing scripts for *The Campbell Playhouse* into the spring of 1939. He later described his time with the Mercury company as "an experience lasting six months I wouldn't have missed nor would want to go through again." In March, he went to Hollywood, too, where he wrote screenplays for the Warner Brothers film studio. In 1944, Koch won an Academy Award as co-screenwriter for the acclaimed film *Casablanca*.

Then, in 1947, Koch's life was upended. A Hollywood producer suggested to the House Un-American Activities Committee that Koch was a Communist. Though no evidence or charges were ever brought against him, the accusation cut short Koch's Hollywood career.

Unable to get work there, he moved to England, where he wrote screenplays under pseudonyms. After a few years, Koch returned to the United States, but his film career had been damaged. Eventually, he was able to make his living again writing screenplays, plays, and books under his own name.

In October 1988, fifty years after the radio broadcast, Koch visited Grovers Mill, the town best known for an event that never happened. In honor of his script, the community made Koch the Grand Marshall of the Martian Parade, the highlight of the *War of the Worlds* anniversary celebration. Other events of the four-day festivities included an alien invader costume contest, a Martian panic bike race, and an alien attack reenactment.

Koch profited from the Martian invasion story. As a former lawyer, he had made a smart legal deal when taking the job with *The Mercury Theatre on the Air* in 1938. In exchange for a low salary, he negotiated with John Houseman and Orson Welles to give him the copyright of any scripts he wrote. After the *War of the Worlds* broadcast, many people and organizations wanted to publish the script. They came to Koch, willing to give him credit and money for his work.

When Welles heard about this, he declared his ownership of the script. Asserting that he had been instrumental in writing it, Welles wanted control of its future use. He lost his lawsuit against Koch when Houseman and Anne Froelick testified that Welles's role in writing the original script had been minimal.

In an interview a few years before his death, Koch said: "I am disappointed in the gullibility of the American people . . . that they accept most outrageous things as truths. . . . I guess there are a lot of schools that don't teach the fundamental things of how to think for yourself. In that aspect, it [the *War of the Worlds* broadcast] was a warning."

Koch died on August 17, 1995, at age ninety-three.

ANNE FROELICK

The young woman who helped Koch with *The War of the Worlds* and other *Mercury Theatre on the Air* scripts also saw her life transformed by the broadcast. In 1939, Anne Froelick followed Koch to Hollywood as his secretary at Warner Brothers.

He recognized her talent and tried to convince the studio to hire her as a writer instead. But her gender proved to be a disadvantage, and Froelick had to work as a secretary for more than a year before Warner Brothers promoted her to writer. She and Koch collaborated on several screenplays, and she was finally given screen credit for her work in 1941. She sometimes wrote as "Anne Froelich."

During the early 1950s, Froelick — like Koch — became a victim of Hollywood's anti-Communist fervor. As a known member of the Communist Party, Froelick had trouble finding work as a screenwriter after 1950. Because of her politics, her husband lost his job at Lockheed, a company with government contracts. In 1953, two other screenwriters reported Froelick to the House Un-American Activities Committee, and she was officially blacklisted.

To overcome this stigma, Froelick used her married name, Anne Taylor, as a pseudonym. Although she later wrote some plays and a novel, her Hollywood career was over. Anne Froelick Taylor died at age ninety-six in January 2010.

This plaque at a park in Grovers Mill, New Jersey, marks the site of the imaginary Martian landing on October 30, 1938.

NOT FORGOTTEN

In May 2016, the last surviving member of the *Mercury*'s *War of the Worlds* team died at age ninety-nine. William Herz had played the parts of two ham-radio operators. His line was one of the most terrifying of the broadcast: "Poisonous black smoke pouring in. . . . Gas masks useless."

Few people are alive who remember hearing the original *Mercury Theatre* program on Sunday night, October 30, 1938. But the "panic broadcast" hasn't been forgotten. Over the decades, it has been the subject of films, plays, TV movies, websites, and numerous books and articles. A bronze plaque at Grovers Mill marks the site of the imaginary Martian landing.

Fortunately, recordings of the broadcast still exist. (See More to Explore, page 110.) Decades later, listeners marvel at the skill of the performances. Frank Readick's perfect imitation of the commentator at the *Hindenburg* explosion. The believability of Kenny Delmar's FDR impersonation. And twenty-three-year-old Orson Welles as the middle-aged astronomy professor facing the end of civilization . . . on the night America was spooked.

HOAXES

"If the nonexistent Martians in the broadcast
had anything important to teach us,
I believe it is the virtue of doubting and
testing everything that comes to us over
the airwaves and on the printed pages."

—Howard Koch

In the wake of the *War of the Worlds* broadcast, many editorials and letter writers echoed Orson Welles's comment, "How are people so silly as to believe the thing like that[!]"

Although the program wasn't intended as a deception, it had elements of a successful hoax. The best ones contain enough truth to seem plausible. Letters and oral accounts from 1938 show that listeners were taken in by the real names of places. Some had heard about life on Mars and accepted that the creatures had come to Earth. Others assumed the invaders were German Nazis.

A hoax can be convincing if its source appears legitimate. The *Mercury* broadcast simulated news bulletins, which radio listeners trusted. Details, such as scientific words and voices of authority figures, sounded genuine.

Hoaxes often play on anxiety and fear. Hitler's aggression in Europe made Americans jittery. Many listeners became afraid when they thought that the United States had been invaded. Some decided to act quickly to save themselves and their families, not stopping to verify what they'd heard on the radio.

Once a person believed in the invasion and became frightened, he or she unconsciously ignored announcements and clues that contradicted that belief. A few people even imagined they smelled poison smoke and saw fire caused by the Martians' heat ray.

The *War of the Worlds* broadcast wasn't the first time—or the last—that a media hoax tricked people.

THE GREAT MOON HOAX

Nineteenth-century newspapers intentionally printed fake news stories to entertain readers and increase sales.

In August 1835, the *New York Sun* published the Great Moon Hoax. It involved a famous astronomer, Sir John Herschel. He was the son of well-known astronomer William Herschel, who earlier had proposed that Mars could support intelligent life.

According to a series of six articles in the *Sun*, Sir John had spotted life on the Moon through his enormous telescope in South Africa. The articles included scientific language and specific details about the telescope's unprecedented power. Many people already thought it was possible for the Moon to support life. The articles convinced them that it was home to bison-like animals, two-legged beavers, flying bat-men, and other strange creatures.

Sir John was a respected scientist, and he really did have a powerful telescope (the plausible part). But most readers didn't know that he never claimed to have seen life on the Moon.

A nineteenth-century illustration of the 1835 Great Moon Hoax. It shows the extraordinary creatures that supposedly lived on the Moon.

The hoax spread when other newspapers throughout the United States and the world reprinted the articles as if they were true. No one could confirm the story with Sir John. In those days, before telegraph and fast ships, it would take months to reach him in South Africa. The hoax wasn't exposed until a few weeks later when its author admitted he'd made it up.

THE CENTRAL PARK ZOO ESCAPE

On a Monday morning in November 1874, the *New York Herald* proclaimed: "Awful Calamity. The Wild Animals Broken Loose from Central Park." A zookeeper's carelessness, the newspaper said, led to the escape of dozens of animals from the Central Park Zoo the day before. A rhinoceros, elephant, panthers, wolves, lions, bears, tigers, monkeys, and dozens of other animals were out of their cages. The creatures were roaming city streets, threatening millions of New Yorkers.

Nearly fifty people had been killed and two hundred injured. The article described the animal attacks in grisly detail and included a list of victims. Although the police

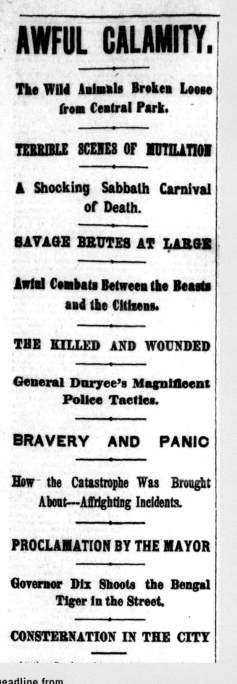

The headline from
the *New York Herald*,
November 9, 1874.
The ten-thousand-word
fake article filled an
entire page.

AWFUL CALAMITY.

The Wild Animals Broken Loose from Central Park.

TERRIBLE SCENES OF MUTILATION

A Shocking Sabbath Carnival of Death.

SAVAGE BRUTES AT LARGE

Awful Combats Between the Beasts and the Citizens.

THE KILLED AND WOUNDED

General Duryee's Magnificent Police Tactics.

BRAVERY AND PANIC

How the Catastrophe Was Brought About---Affrighting Incidents.

PROCLAMATION BY THE MAYOR

Governor Dix Shoots the Bengal Tiger in the Street.

CONSTERNATION IN THE CITY

and even the governor had shot and killed many of the beasts, a dozen were still at large.

The story was persuasive. New Yorkers knew the Central Park Zoo was home to dangerous wild animals, and the article played to the fear of them. Officials were quoted and victims named, making the story more believable.

The final paragraph of the ten-thousand-word piece stated: "Not one word of it is true. Not a single act or incident described has taken place. It is a huge hoax."

Many readers never saw the disclaimer. Long before reaching the end of the page, they panicked. Parents ran to find children who had just left for school, dragging them home to safety. Armed men took to the streets to hunt down the animals.

The *Herald* later admitted creating the hoax to bring attention to inadequate safety at the zoo. The newspaper's editors never imagined that anyone would fall for it.

GOING VIRAL

Today, hoaxes appear on the Internet, reaching more people faster than was ever possible with newspapers.

In 2014, a story circulated for two days about a pregnant pet tarantula named Penelope. A "Missing" sign with her picture was taped to a pole in Brooklyn, New York, asking for help finding her.

People in the area felt uncomfortable about a poisonous spider wandering their neighborhood, and blogs discussed the dangers posed by Penelope and her offspring. A passerby submitted a picture of the sign to social media website Reddit, and the news spread farther. ABC tweeted it. The *New York Times* and *New York Daily News* covered the story.

There was no Penelope the tarantula. A man had put up the sign as a joke, poking fun at the missing cat and dog posters he often saw. Thanks to social media, it was a prank that spiraled out of control.

ZAP AND DRILL

In 2014, a fake online Apple advertisement went viral, fooling a few iPhone users. It explained that the latest operating system enabled owners to charge their phones by placing them in a microwave oven. The ad looked like one of Apple's, and the scientific description of the process sounded authentic: "synchronize with microwave frequencies and use them to recharge your battery."

When Apple introduced the iPhone 7 in September 2016, it lacked a headphone jack. Within days, a hoax appeared on the Internet with a fix for customers upset about the change. The jack was there, but Apple had hidden it beneath the case. All you had to do to access the jack was to drill through the case at the correct point. A YouTube video showed how. Millions viewed the video. Some of them drilled the hole . . . and destroyed their phone.

EXPLOSION AT THE WHITE HOUSE

In April 2013, one of the Associated Press Twitter accounts sent out the message: "Breaking: Two Explosions in the White House and Barack Obama is injured." Within minutes, the nation's financial markets reacted. Stock prices and the dollar's value dropped sharply as investors anticipated a national crisis.

Realizing that its account had been hacked, the AP quickly took down the false message. The news service announced on Facebook and its newswire that the tweet was fake. Several minutes later, an AP reporter repeated the denial at a White House press conference. The president's press secretary and the roomful of reporters sitting unharmed could confirm that there had been no explosions.

As soon as word of the hack broke, the markets bounced back to normal levels. The episode lasted less than ten minutes. But it revealed how fake news from a legitimate source could tear through social media and cause serious repercussions.

See More to Explore (page 110) to read about other memorable hoaxes.

 The Associated Press ✔
@AP

Breaking: Two Explosions in the White House and Barack Obama is injured

The fake Associated Press tweet from April 23, 2013

TIMELINE

1866
September 21—
H. G. Wells born
in England.

Orson Welles and
H. G. Wells meet.

Princeton Radio
Research Project
publishes its study of
the reaction to the
War of the Worlds
broadcast.

March—Hitler's Germany takes
over Austria.

July—The Mercury broadcasts its
first radio drama.

1946   **1940**   **1939-1945**   ⚡   **1938** ⚡

August 13—
H. G. Wells dies.

World War II.

September—Hurricane devastates
the northeastern U.S.

October—Hitler's Germany takes
over part of Czechoslovakia.

Howard Koch joins the Mercury.

October 30—*The Mercury
Theatre on the Air* presents
The War of the Worlds.

December—*The Campbell
Playhouse* debuts.

1985

October 10—
Orson Welles dies.

1988

October—
Grovers Mill celebrates
fiftieth anniversary of
the *War of the Worlds*
broadcast.

October 31—
John Houseman dies.

The War of the Worlds published in *Pearson's Magazine*.

September 22— John Houseman born in Romania.

World War I.

1895   1897   1898   1901   1902   1914–1918

Percival Lowell publishes book claiming that Mars is inhabited by an advanced civilization.

The War of the Worlds released as a novel.

December 12— Howard Koch born in New York.

May 6— Orson Welles born in Wisconsin. **1915**

Houseman and Welles stage plays for Federal Theatre Project.

January— John Houseman and Orson Welles meet.

March— Charles Lindbergh's son kidnapped in New Jersey.

1937   1936–1937   1935   1933   1932   1929

Houseman and Welles establish the Mercury Theatre.

May—German airship *Hindenburg* explodes in Lakehurst, New Jersey, killing thirty-six.

January— Adolf Hitler becomes chancellor of Germany.

March— Franklin Roosevelt becomes president of the U.S. and delivers his first radio fireside chat.

October— Stock market crashes; U.S. plunges into the Great Depression.

1995   2010   2016

August 17— Howard Koch dies.

January 26— Anne Froelick dies.

May 10— William Herz, last surviving member of the *War of the Worlds* broadcast, dies.

MORE TO EXPLORE*

> "It is impossible to sit in a room and hear the scratched, worn, off-the-air recording of the broadcast, without feeling in the back of your neck some slight draft left over from that great wind of terror that swept the nation."
>
> —*John Houseman*

THE WAR OF THE WORLDS

THE RADIO BROADCAST AND SCRIPT

"'War of the Worlds' 1938 Radio Broadcast."
YouTube.
youtube.com/watch?v=OzC3Fg_rRJM
    Listen to the October 30, 1938, *War of the Worlds* program, posted by the Newseum.

The full October 30, 1938, broadcast is also available at:

"Orson Welles—Mercury Theater-1938 recordings."
Internet Archive.
archive.org/details/OrsonWelles-MercuryTheater-1938Recordings
    In addition to *The War of the Worlds*, the site contains more than a dozen other *Mercury* broadcasts. Also included is "Mercury Theater Remembered" from the 1988 recording *Theatre of the Imagination: The Mercury Company Remembers*. This production includes comments by Orson Welles, John Houseman, Bernard Herrmann, and several Mercury actors about the *War of the Worlds* broadcast.

Websites active at time of publication

"Orson Welles' 'The War of the Worlds' radio drama—CBS October 30, 1938—subtitled."
YouTube.
youtube.com/watch?v=oWD9Q6klzco
   This YouTube version includes photographs and illustrations.

"Mercury Theatre, War of the Worlds, Oct 30 1938."
Generic Radio Workshop Script Library.
genericradio.com/show.php?id=3e128b5a5d82a7fc
   Read the script written by Howard Koch. It differs from the actual recording because of minor changes made during rehearsals and the broadcast.

THE REACTION

"Orson Welles apologizes for The War of the Worlds' mass panic."
YouTube.
youtube.com/watch?v=8vbYyDh-BRI
   Watch the press conference held the day after the famous broadcast. At the end, hear two versions of Welles's prepared statement.

"'Attack By Mars' Panic; Orson Wells [*sic*] Speaks 1938/10/31."
YouTube.
youtube.com/watch?v=ho_9XTnlJKM
   This edited Universal Newsreel version of Welles's prepared statement was shown in movie theaters. It is a third version of the prepared statement.

"AT&T Operators Recall War of the Worlds Broadcast."
YouTube.
youtube.com/watch?v=R29BTsoIHpQ&index=10&list=PLWocaE3xRbeqMox
fTAWazPJhUda6Usxle

From the AT&T Tech Channel, AT&T operators from across the country tell how phone customers reacted to the October 30, 1938, broadcast.

"Orson Wells [*sic*] Meets H. G. Wells."
YouTube.
youtube.com/watch?v=nUdghSMTXsU

Listen to the 1940 broadcast of the two men discussing *The War of the Worlds* at Texas radio station KTSA, San Antonio.

LOOKING BACK

***American Experience*: "War of the Worlds" (DVD).**
PBS, 2013.

This documentary covers the famous 1938 broadcast using actors, archival radio and video recordings, photographs, and interviews.

"*American Experience*: War of the Worlds" (website).
PBS and WGBH Educational Foundation.
pbs.org/wgbh/americanexperience/features/introduction/worlds/

The website for the *American Experience* DVD includes video and audio clips from the documentary, the complete transcript, a timeline of 1930s news, photographs, and books and websites for further reading.

"War of the Worlds."
Radiolab.
radiolab.org/story/91622-war-of-the-worlds

Hear excerpts from the 1938 *Mercury Theatre* show. Listen to a discussion about the original broadcast, later imitations, and the public reaction to them.

"War of the Worlds Radio Documentary from October 30, 1988, Parts 1 and 2."
YouTube.
youtube.com/watch?v=ol3NRuMOEGk
youtube.com/watch?v=s7811lx10y4

NPR's radio documentary aired on October 30, 1988, marking the fiftieth anniversary of the famous broadcast. It includes interviews with several people involved in the program.

Whig Hill School,
Rockford, Ill.
Nov. 21, 1938.

Federal Communications Commission,
Washington, D.C.
Gentlemen:
This was that I thought of
story of World War of the Martians written
by Orson Welles.
I thought it was a good story and
wanted to hear it a gane. It did not scare
me. I'm 12 years old.

Yours truly,
Merritt H. Junior Swick

VPB2 34 NL

MEADVILLE PENN 30

FEDERAL COMMUNICATIONS COMMISSION   44-3   WAR OF THE WOR

WASHN DC

SUNDAY NIGHT MERCURY THEATRE OF AIR NOT ONLY IN BAD TASTE BUT
DANGEROUS STOP MY WIFE AND SEVERAL OTHER WOMEN CONFINED TO BEDS
FROM SHOCK AND HYSTERIA STOP I MAY SUE COLUMBIA BROADCASTING
SYSTEM

CLAUDE L. STEWART.

Orson Welles in 1938

ORSON WELLES

Magician: The Astonishing Life and Work of Orson Welles **(DVD).**
Cohen Media Group, 2014.

This biographical documentary covers Welles's career, including the *War of the Worlds* radio broadcast. Watch Welles talking about his life, interviews with people who knew him, and excerpts from his movies and performances.

1930s RADIO

"The Broadcast News."
Radio Days.
otr.com/news.html#events

Listen to several alarming news broadcasts from 1938, listed under "Hitler Seizes Austria!" and "Hitler Wants Territory."

"Herbert Morrison—WLS Radio (Chicago) Address on the Hindenburg Disaster."
AmericanRhetoric, Online Speech Bank.
americanrhetoric.com/speeches/hindenburgcrash.htm

The site features part of the recording made by reporter Herbert Morrison on May 6, 1937, as the German passenger zeppelin *Hindenburg* exploded upon arriving in Lakehurst, New Jersey. His emotional reaction to the explosion inspired actor Frank Readick to copy Morrison's voice in the *War of the Worlds* radio broadcast. Both audio and the transcript of Morrison's broadcast are included.

To hear the entire thirty-six-minute version of Morrison's broadcast (with the airship's explosion occurring at the 8:32 mark), visit: "Hindenburg Disaster."
Radio Days.
otr.com/hindenburg.shtml

The radio in a Missouri home, 1938

"Franklin Delano Roosevelt, First Fireside Chat."
AmericanRhetoric, Online Speech Bank.
americanrhetoric.com/mp3clips/politicalspeeches/fdrfirstfiresidechat63496436943.
mp3

Listen to President Franklin Roosevelt's first radio fireside chat, delivered on March 12, 1933. Actor Kenny Delmar imitated FDR's voice during the *War of the Worlds* broadcast.

"The March of Time."
Radio Days.

otr.com/march.html

The radio program *The March of Time* dramatized news events. Click on the blue links to hear the shows about the Lindbergh baby's 1932 kidnapping and the 1941 bombing of Pearl Harbor. Orson Welles and other Mercury Theatre actors had roles on this radio program, and Ora Nichols provided sound effects.

"Introduction to Foley and Sound Effects for Film."
YouTube.

youtube.com/watch?v=_Jznye0iqYE

During the 1930s, sound effects were produced live while a radio program aired. Today, sound effects are added to movies after filming ends. These sounds are created using the Foley technique. This video by FilmmakerIQ.com includes a look at a radio-drama performance with the actors and sound effects experts gathered around microphones. Learn how sound effects are created for films today, using many of the tricks from radio days.

MARS

"Mars Exploration."
NASA.

mars.nasa.gov

Find out about the latest Mars discoveries and the space agency's views on life, water, and "canals" on the planet. Ask questions of NASA's computerized scientist, Dr. C., at mars.nasa.gov/drc/. View images and video of Mars at mars.nasa.gov/multimedia/.

NASA's Mars rover *Curiosity* takes a selfie on the Mars surface in 2015.

HOAXES

The Museum of Hoaxes.
hoaxes.org
   Check out a collection of hoaxes and pranks from the Middle Ages to the present. Meet the clever pranksters who fooled scientists, journalists, and historians, as well as the general public.

A Colorful History of Popular Delusions **by Robert E. Bartholomew and Peter Hassall.** Amherst, NY: Prometheus Books, 2015.
   Read about past and present cases of mass delusion, panic, and hysteria. Learn how rumor, urban legends, and social media lead to false beliefs and fears.

Media Hoaxes **by Fred Fedler.** Ames: Iowa State University Press, 1989.
   Find out about successful hoaxes that appeared in newspapers, radio, and television. Discover a few famous ones that people still believe more than a hundred years later.

Real or Fake?: Far-Out Fibs, Fishy Facts, and Phony Photos to Test for the Truth **by Emily Krieger.** Washington, DC: National Geographic Kids, 2016.
   How gullible are you? Test your skill at spotting lies and deceptions among dozens of examples. A nonfiction book for young readers.

The Giant and How He Humbugged America **by Jim Murphy.** New York: Scholastic, 2012.
   The true story of the Cardiff Giant hoax in upstate New York, 1869. A nonfiction book for young readers.

FICTION

The War of the Worlds **by H. G. Wells.** New York: Harper, 1898.
catalog.hathitrust.org/Record/012293655
   The novel is widely available in print and online.

The Tripods series by John Christopher. New York: Aladdin, 1967–1988.
   This series of novels for young adults depicts Earth invaded by extraterrestrials who use machines called Tripods, similar to those in H. G. Wells's novel.

Author's Note

My first step in researching this book was to listen to a recording of the *War of the Worlds* radio broadcast. Since that day, I have played it so many times that I've lost count. Parts of it still give me goose bumps.

Next, I studied H. G. Wells's story to identify the ways that Howard Koch and *The Mercury Theatre* adapted the original version.

In writing the two chapters that recounted the radio play, I relied on the words people heard in their homes that night in 1938. Published versions of the script differ in small ways from what went out over the airwaves. (For links to the broadcast, see More to Explore, page 110.)

The scenes included in this book are based on primary source materials. I have not embellished anecdotes or invented dialogue. I didn't need to. The memoirs, correspondence, and eyewitness accounts by the people who lived through the *War of the Worlds* broadcast are fascinating enough. Photographs and film clips of characters and events helped me describe key moments. (For direct quotations, see Source Notes, page 120. For primary sources, see starred entries in the Selected Bibliography, page 131.)

After reading the first chapter of *Spooked!*, you might have thought the Nazis or another enemy had once invaded the United States. If so, you got a taste of how radio listeners felt that Halloween Eve.

Orson Welles and the *Mercury Theatre* team intended to tell an entertaining story, never expecting the listeners' reactions. For some people, fear and survival instincts took over. They prepared to escape. They called their friends to warn them. They pounded on the neighbors' doors. They ran out into the streets crying, "Martians have landed!" But they didn't confirm that the radio bulletins were true. Instead, they spread the word.

This is not so different from sharing a social media post without checking its accuracy.

Today, we are regularly bombarded with messages designed to persuade us. Scammers, advertisers, and political and special interest groups use media of all kinds to influence our actions and opinions. Sometimes, so do our friends.

Many online news sites mix genuine news stories with "sponsored content" that looks like a news article but is actually advertising. Numerous groups and individuals post fake news that is meant to be satirical and amusing. Other hoaxers invent articles and headlines, encouraging us to share them. That drives Internet traffic to their sites and earns them advertising money.

It isn't easy to pick out those who are tricking us for selfish or malicious reasons. The best we can do is to question what we see and hear, to verify the accuracy if possible, and to avoid jumping to conclusions. Does the statement make sense? Is it exaggerated or misleading? Is it gossip? Is it propaganda? What is the source of the information? Is that source reliable? What is its point of view or agenda?

Listen to the *War of the Worlds* radio broadcast. Better yet, listen with your eyes closed or the lights off. Would you have believed that Martians were attacking? Would you have panicked? Or would you have said, "This is a wonderfully scary Halloween story!"?

—GJ

Source Notes*

The source of each quotation in this book is found below. The citation indicates the first words of the quotation and its document source. The sources are listed either in the bibliography or below.

The following abbreviations are used:

MERC—*Theatre of the Imagination: The Mercury Company Remembers*, sound recording produced by Frank Beacham

MICH—Richard Wilson-Orson Welles Papers, University of Michigan

NARA—General Correspondence 1927–1946, Federal Communications Commission (FCC), National Archives

RADIO—*The War of the Worlds* radio broadcast, October 30, 1938

WELLS—*The War of the Worlds* by H. G. Wells, 1898

CHAPTER ONE   HAUNTED ON HALLOWEEN EVE (page 9)

"We figured our friends . . .": college student, quoted in Cantril, pp. 51–52.

"shock of almost . . .": RADIO.

"They wrecked . . .": same as above.

CHAPTER TWO   MERCURY RISES (page 14)

"From the day . . .": Roger Hill, quoted in "People," *Time*, December 5, 1938, p. 60.

"a reputation . . .": Houseman, *Run-Through*, p. 128.

"Would you like . . .": Houseman, interview with Simon Callow, n.d., MICH, box 16.

"[taking] possession . . .": "S.R.O. for the WPA," by Brooks Atkinson, *New York Times*, January 31, 1937.

"Cartoonist, Actor . . .": "Cartoonist, Actor, Poet and only 10," *Capital Times* [Madison, WI], February 19, 1926.

"Everybody told me . . .": Welles, quoted in Estrin, p. 179.

"The theatre was . . .": Hascy Tarbox, quoted in Callow, p. 44.

"Although he is . . .": "This Ageless Soul," by Russell Maloney, *The New Yorker*, October 8, 1938, p. 22.

"He was capable . . .": Houseman, *Run-Through*, p. 362.

"an exciting excursion . . .": "Mercury Theatre Opens With a Version of 'Julius Caesar' in Modern Dress," by Brooks Atkinson, *New York Times*, November 12, 1937.

"innate dramatic . . .": Houseman, *Run-Through*, p. 170.

"Very few . . ." and "He was difficult": Arlene Francis, interview with Frank Beacham, February 26, 1988, MICH, box 14.

"the brightest moon . . .": "Marvelous Boy," *Time*, May 9, 1938, p. 36.

CHAPTER THREE **TAKING TO THE AIR** (page 21)

"Before we know . . .": *Stockton* [CA] *Record*, quoted in "Bravos from the Nation's Press," *Broadcasting*, August 15, 1938, p. 7.

"the brightest sensation . . .": "Columbia sets the stage . . . and action is the cue!," *Broadcasting*, August 15, 1938, p. 6.

"Bernard Herrmann knew . . .": William Alland, MERC.

"conditions of . . .": Houseman, "The Men from Mars," p. 75.

"I had to either . . ." and "I decided . . .": Koch, *As Time Goes By*, p. 39.

"tireless . . .": Houseman, in foreword of same as above, p. xiii.

"What do you like . . .": Houseman, interview with Leonard Maltin, April 22, 1988, MICH, box 14.

CHAPTER FOUR **BLOOD-RED PLANET** (page 25)

"The world went . . .": WELLS, p. 8.

"I'm doing . . .": letter from Wells to Elizabeth Healey, late spring 1896, in Smith, p. 261.

"a morning star . . .": WELLS, p. 5.

"Slowly and surely . . .": same as above, p. 4.

"long, flexible . . .": same as above, p. 71.

"merely heads": same as above, p. 205.

"the size . . .": same as above, p. 28.

"about four feet . . .": same as above, p. 203.

"luminous": same as above, p. 28.

"whip-like . . .": same as above, p. 204.

"gray snake": same as above, p. 28.

"The main road . . .": same as above, p. 158.

"men choking . . .": same as above, p. 146.

"boilers . . .": same as above, p. 128.

"Certainly what we see . . .": Lowell, p. 209.

"What manner of beings . . .": same as above, p. 211.

CHAPTER FIVE **PLOTTING THE INVASION** (page 29)

"No one . . .": Houseman, "The Men from Mars," p. 75.

"We can only . . ." and "It is almost certain . . .": Pickering, quoted in "Mars Poses Its Riddle of Life," by H. Gordon Garbedian, *New York Times*, December 9, 1928.

"That there may ...": "The Week in Science: Life at Minus 40 Degrees," by Waldemar Kaempffert, *New York Times*, January 12, 1936.

"John, what ...": Koch, quoted by Houseman, interview with Leonard Maltin, April 22, 1988, MICH, box 14.

"authentic ring": Koch, *The Panic Broadcast*, p. 13.

"You can't ..." and "Those old Martians ...": Froelick, quoted by Houseman in "The Men from Mars," p. 76.

"moves and ...": Koch, *The Panic Broadcast*, p. 15.

"I can hear it ...": Welles, quoted in Johnston and Smith, February 3, 1940, p. 27.

"Nobody's going ...": William Herz, quoted in "After Nearly 80 Years, Still Coming to Sardi's," by Manny Fernandez, *New York Times*, May 25, 2010.

"lousy" and "Don't bother ..." and "Probably bore ...": actor, quoted in Gross, p. 197.

"We agreed ...": Houseman, "The Men from Mars," p. 76.

CHAPTER SIX THE FINAL DAY (page 34)

"Everybody likes ...": Welles, *The Campbell Playhouse* episode *Rebecca*, radio broadcast, December 9, 1938.

"We had done ...": Houseman, *Run-Through*, p. 393.

"Very dull ...": sound technician, quoted by Welles in Johnston and Smith, February 3, 1940, p. 27.

"so silly ...": Welles, quoted by Richard Barr in Callow, p. 400.

"He could give ...": Arthur Anderson, quoted in Maltin, p. 79.

"Sweating ...": Houseman, *Run-Through*, p. 391.

"Oh Kenny ...": Welles, quoted by Kenny Delmar in *The War of the Worlds* ..., Sourcebooks, p. 20.

"That was the only ...": Houseman, quoted in same as above.

"There [will] not ...": Houseman, *Run-Through*, p. 402.

"How we got ...": Stewart, interview with Francois Thomas, March 29, 1982, MICH, box 17.

"a strange fever ...": Houseman, *Run-Through*, p. 398.

CHAPTER SEVEN THE ATTACK (page 40)

"It was the beginning ...": WELLS, p. 170.

"envious eyes": RADIO.

"incandescent gas" and "spectroscope": same as above.

"Not canals ...": same as above.

"I'd say ...": same as above.

"A safe enough ...": same as above.

"At 8:50 ...": same as above.

"We take you ...": same as above.

"Mr. Wilmuth ...": same as above.

"I seen ...": same as above.

"I don't know ...": same as above.

"Something's happening!": same as above.

"Keep back . . .": same as above.

"This is the most . . ." through "I can hardly . . .": same as above.

"A humped shape . . ." and "Good Lord . . .": same as above.

"It's coming . . .": same as above.

"At least forty . . .": same as above.

"scientific knowledge . . .": same as above.

"absolute nonconductivity . . .": same as above.

"The charred . . .": same as above.

"It's something moving . . ." through "Hold on!": same as above.

"Ladies and gentlemen . . .": same as above.

"crushed . . .": same as above.

"I shall not . . ." and "confined . . .": same as above.

CHAPTER EIGHT PANIC (page 52)

"The Martians are coming!": WELLS, p. 162.

"Martians have landed": New Jersey resident, quoted by Lolly MacKenzie Dey in
"Local residents recall 1938 Martian Panic," by Bill Sanservino, *West Windsor
Chronicle, WOW 50th Preview & Guide*, October 20, 1988.

"The Martians are invading . . .": CBS operators, quoted by Hal Davies in *War of the
Worlds with Orson Wells* [*sic*], NPR Radio Documentary, from October 30, 1988,
Part 1, YouTube, youtube.com/watch?v=ol3NRuMOEGk.

"Don't panic . . .": Hal Davies, quoted in Gosling, p. 46.

"A terrible thing . . .": phone call, quoted by Paley in *War of the Worlds with Orson Wells*
[*sic*], NPR Radio Documentary, from October 30, 1988, Part 1, YouTube,
youtube.com/watch?v=ol3NRuMOEGk.

"Martians have landed . . .": New Jersey resident, quoted by Lolly MacKenzie Dey
in *West Windsor Chronicle, WOW 50th Preview & Guide*, October 20, 1988.

"A rocket is . . .": woman, quoted by Mary Congelo in letter to Welles, n.d., MICH, box 24.

"spellbound" and "scared . . .": letter from Emmet F. Riordan to Welles,
October 30, 1938, MICH, box 24.

"friends and families . . ." through "I thought the . . .": college student, quoted in
Cantril, pp. 51–52.

"I sat on the . . .": letter from Dean Livingston to *Mercury Theatre of the Air*,
October 30, 1938, MICH, box 24.

"So much has . . .": letter from Edith B. Slack to Frank R. McNinch, November 1, 1938,
NARA, box 238.

"Professors . . .": letter from S. L. Williams to FCC, November 1, 1938, NARA, box 238.

CHAPTER NINE "WRECKAGE" (page 56)

"Wreckage": WELLS, chapter title, p. 283.

"People were fighting . . .": WELLS, p. 148.

"You've got to stop . . .": Davidson Taylor, quoted by Houseman, interview with
   Leonard Maltin, April 22, 1988, MICH, box 14.
"No! No! . . .": Houseman, same as above.
"Bulletins too numerous . . .": RADIO.
"is to crush resistance . . .": same as above.
"Green flash! . . .": same as above.
"Eight army bombers . . .": same as above.
"Poisonous black . . .": same as above.
"Artillery . . ." and "This may be . . .": same as above.
"This is the end . . .": same as above.
"like flies" and "like rats": same as above.
"Isn't there . . .": same as above.
"They wrecked . . .": same as above.
"We're eatable . . .": same as above.
"Stark and silent . . .": same as above.
"the Mercury Theatre's . . .": same as above.
"If your doorbell . . .": same as above.

CHAPTER TEN IT'S ALL OVER (page 67)
"We all felt . . .": radio listener, quoted in Cantril, p. 98.
"Oh Mother, . . .": letter from Josephine O'Cone to Welles, October 31, 1938, MICH, box 24.
"one horrible . . .": letter from Estelle Paultz to Welles, October 1938, MICH, box 24.
"fearful monster" and "suffered agony": letter from Thomas Brosnan to the secretary
   of the interior, November 2, 1938, NARA, box 238.
"In this day . . .": letter from Hugh Weatherlow to the Federal Radio Commission,
   October 31, 1938, NARA, box 238.
"fools together . . .": letter from Mrs. William Drumheller to Welles, October 30, 1938,
   MICH, box 24.
"I bet . . .": Mrs. Weeden, quoted by George Weeden in letter to Mercury Theatre,
   October 30, 1938, MICH, box 24.
"For a Halloween . . .": letter from George Weeden, same as above.
"I never have . . .": letter from Robert Keplinger to Welles, October 30, 1938, MICH, box 23.
"If you and your cast . . .": letter from Esther Burlingame to Columbia Broadcasting
   Company, October 30, 1938, MICH, box 24.
"I do know . . .": letter from Gerta S. Brown to Mercury Theater, November 2, 1938,
   MICH, box 24.
"electricity . . .": boy, quoted in letter from Theodore Wegener to McNinch, NARA, box 238.
"very much irritated . . .": letter from Wegener to McNinch, same as above.
"betrayed itself" and "I . . . do not . . .": letter from John S. Borg to Columbia Broadcasting
   System, October 30, 1938, NARA, box 238.
"Mars had cracked . . .": man, quoted by Thomas E. Rhodes in letter to McNinch,
   October 31, 1938, NARA, box 238.

"crippled" and "paralyzed": letter from Paul Morton to FCC, October 31, 1938, NARA, box 238.

"would-be…":"Hoax Spreads Terror Here; Some Pack Up," Trenton [NJ] Evening Times, October 31, 1938.

"was dead…": Koch, interview with Joe Bevilacqua, We Take You Now to Grover's Mill: The Making of the "War of the Worlds" Broadcast.

"If this is a joke…": official, quoted by Houseman, interview with Leonard Maltin, April 22, 1988, MICH, box 14.

"Nobody was…": Houseman, "The Men from Mars," p. 74.

"We believed…": Houseman, interview with Leonard Maltin, April 22, 1988, MICH, box 14.

"entirely fictitious": Columbia system, quoted in "Radio Play Terrifies Nation," Boston Daily Globe, October 31, 1938.

"jammed with…": "Mass Hysteria Is Result of Play Broadcast in U.S.," Dunkirk [NY] Evening Observer, October 31, 1938.

"I don't know what's…" and "How are people…": Welles, quoted by Arlene Francis, MERC.

CHAPTER ELEVEN EXTRA! EXTRA! READ ALL ABOUT IT! (page 74)

"Radio Drama…": Ogdensburg [NY] Journal, October 31, 1938.

"Invasion" and "Panic": passersby, quoted in Koch, As Time Goes By, p. 7.

"Haven't you…": barber, quoted in same as above.

"Nation in Panic…": newspaper, quoted in same as above.

"Men, women…": Koch, The Panic Broadcast, p. 11.

"the wave of…": "U.S. Investigates Radio Drama of Invasion by Martians That Threw Nation Into Panic," New York World-Telegram, October 31, 1938.

"Monsters of…": by Marshall Andrews, Washington Post, October 31, 1938.

"Hoax Spreads…": Trenton [NJ] Evening Times, October 31, 1938.

"Radio Listeners…": New York Times, October 31, 1938.

"Many Fear…": Boston Daily Globe, October 31, 1938.

"disregarding…":"U.S. Investigates Radio Drama of Invasion by Martians That Threw Nation Into Panic," New York World-Telegram, October 31, 1938.

"Hundreds": "Radio Listeners in Panic, Taking War Drama as Fact," New York Times, October 31, 1938.

"at least a score": same as above.

"many were injured…": "Too-Real Radio Drama Gives Nation a Bad Case of War Jitters," Dunkirk [NY]Evening Observer, November 1, 1938.

"casualty": same as above.

"victim": "Fake Radio 'War' Stirs Terror Through U.S.," New York Daily News, October 31, 1938.

"What time will…": caller, quoted in "Radio Listeners in Panic, Taking War Drama as Fact," New York Times, October 31, 1938.

"so that the city . . .": callers from Providence, RI, quoted in same as above.

"war scare": "What German Press Made of U.S. Scare," *New York Sun*, October 31, 1938.

"Death Ray . . ." and "American People . . .": same as above.

"MILLIONS . . .": "The Editor Says," *New York Journal and American*, November 1, 1938, quoted in Campbell, p. 41.

"epidemic of fear . . .": "U.S. Investigates Radio Drama of Invasion by Martians That Threw Nation Into Panic," *New York World-Telegram*, October 31, 1938.

"suffered a heart . . .": letter from Olive M. Racker, R.N., to War of the Worlds Program, October 31, 1938, MICH, box 23.

"When the announcer . . .": radio listener, quoted in Cantril, p. 100.

"Deeply regretful": Welles, "Orson Welles apologizes for The War of the Worlds' mass panic," YouTube, youtube.com/watch?v=8vbYyDh-BRI.

"deeply concerned": literary representative for H. G. Wells, quoted in "Panic Caused by Broadcast," *The* [London] *Times*, November 1, 1938.

"mistook . . .": W. B. Lewis, quoted in "Divided Reaction to Mars Broadcast," *Broadcasting*, November 15, 1938, p. 28.

"a simulated news . . .": same as above.

"to fulfill . . .": Neville Miller, quoted in same as above.

"Of course, we . . .": Welles, "Orson Welles apologizes for The War of the Worlds' mass panic," YouTube, youtube.com/watch?v=8vbYyDh-BRI.

"It came rather . . .": Welles, YouTube, same as above.

"people might . . .": Welles, quoted in "Radio Listeners in Panic, Taking War Drama as Fact," *New York Times*, October 31, 1938.

"authentic . . .": reporter, "Orson Welles apologizes for The War of the Worlds' mass panic," YouTube, youtube.com/watch?v=8vbYyDh-BRI.

"It would seem . . .": Welles, YouTube, same as above.

"know what the . . .": Welles, YouTube, same as above.

DEAR MR. WELLES (page 80)

"I listened . . .": letter from D. G. Riperton to Welles, n.d., MICH, box 23.

"Personally, I'd rather . . .": letter from Mabel P. Keane to Welles, October 30, 1938, MICH, box 23.

"The American public . . .": letter from Jerome Stone to Welles, n.d., MICH, box 23.

"I have been chosen . . .": letter from Nicholas Carr to Welles, October 31, 1938, MICH, box 23.

"I sincerely hope . . .": letter from Marjorie Nicol to Welles, November 4, 1938, MICH, box 23.

"Mr. Hitler . . .": letter from Mrs. G. Herbert Taylor to Welles, November 1, 1938, MICH, box 24.

"It is a good thing . . .": letter from Helen Louise Spencer and A. W. Hill to Columbia Broadcasting Company, *Mercury Theatre of the Air*, October 30, 1938, MICH, box 23.

"Despite the fact . . .": letter from Monica Harmon to Welles, October 31, 1938, MICH, box 24.

"Aren't you ashamed . . .": letter from Esther Belville to H. B. Wells [*sic*]—C.B.S., October 31, 1938, MICH, box 23.

"Orchids to you . . .": letter from Robert W. Waters, Jr., to Welles, November 1, 1938, MICH, box 23.

"We trust . . .": letter from Mr. and Mrs. Fred L. Hipp to *Mercury Theatre of the Air*, October 31, 1938, MICH, box 24.

"If what I think . . .": letter from Martin Zeller to Mercury Theatre, October 31, 1938, MICH, box 24.

"These mollicoddled . . .": letter from Mrs. S. Shirley to CBS—Detroit—for Mercury Theatre, November 1, 1938, MICH, box 23.

"Perhaps if you'd . . .": letter from Margaret B. McLean to Columbia Broadcasting System, October 31, 1938, MICH, box 24.

"I think the safest . . .": letter from George E. Harris to Welles, October 31, 1938, MICH, box 23.

"There was only one . . .": letter from Miss D. Holstein to Welles, October 31, 1938, MICH, box 24.

"Don't people . . .": letter from E. D. Collins to Welles, n.d., MICH, box 23.

"You have made radio . . .": letter from Merle J. Jennings to Radio Station WBBM, Chicago, October 30, 1938, MICH, box 23.

"It shakes . . .": letter from Daniel O'Grady to Welles, October 31, 1938, MICH, box 23.

"The infernal . . .": letter from Peter Van Wyk to Welles, October 31, 1938, MICH, box 24.

"All this goes . . .": letter from Rachel J. Inman to Welles, October 30, 1938, MICH, box 24.

CHAPTER TWELVE FALLOUT (page 83)

"This only goes . . .": telegram from Alexander Woollcott to Orson Welles, October 30, 1938, quoted in Rosenbaum, p. 18.

"such abuses" and "Radio has no . . .": Herring, quoted in "Drama Terrorizes Thousands: Listeners Believe U.S. Attacked by Mars Men; Congress Probe Demanded," by Charles A. Grumich, *Ogdensburg* [NY] *Journal*, October 31, 1938.

"Any broadcast . . .": McNinch, quoted in "Divided Reaction to Mars Broadcast," *Broadcasting*, November 15, 1938, p. 28.

"The public . . .": T. A. M. Craven, quoted in same as above.

"We don't agree . . .": "Frighted with False Fire," *New York World-Telegram*, November 1, 1938, in Koch, *The Panic Broadcast*, p. 17.

"for spreading . . ." and "a healthy . . .": "Radio and Skepticism," by Uncle Dudley, *Boston Daily Globe*, November 1, 1938.

"shown up the . . ." and "incite hatreds . . .": "On the Record: Mr. Welles and Mass Delusion," by Dorothy Thompson, *New York Herald Tribune*, November 2, 1938.

"The course of . . .": "The Nutsy Happens," by Heywood Broun, *Charlotte* [NC] *News*, November 5, 1938.

"Here is a nation . . .": "Panic Caused by Broadcast," *The* [London] *Times*, November 1, 1938.

"So long as radio . . .": "Calm After The Storm," *Washington Post*, November 2, 1938.

"What began . . ." and "Radio is new . . .": "Terror by Radio," *New York Times*,
    November 1, 1938.
"Who was I . . .": letter from Mrs. M. W. Durham to McNinch, n.d., NARA, box 238.
"the prestige . . .": letter from B. Paul Heritage to FCC, October 31, 1938, NARA, box 238.
"'News Bulletin' . . .": telegram from Kendall B. McClure to McNinch, October 31, 1938,
    NARA, box 238.
"The freedom . . .": letter from H. O. Bergdahl to McNinch, November 3, 1938, NARA,
    box 237.
"It isn't his . . .": postcard from Grace Busse to McNinch, n.d., NARA, box 237.
"radio stations . . ." and "providing jobs . . .": letter to the editor from George C. Wetmore,
    "The People's Forum," *Norwalk* [CT] *Hour*, October 31, 1938.
"Leave the listening . . .": letter to the editor from A. Hoefle, "Letters," *Time*,
    November 21, 1938.
"by studying . . .": letter from Esther Langman to Welles, October 31, 1938, MICH, box 23.
"not only highly . . .": letter from Fanny Lee Winningham to Welles, October 31, 1938,
    MICH, box 23.
"so much static . . .": letter from Maud Rankin Wales to McNinch, November 7, 1938,
    NARA, box 237.
"that the entire land . . ." and "within a few . . .": letter from George B. Wright to
    McNinch, November 1, 1938, NARA, box 237.
"sufficient to protect . . .": "All's Welles That Ends Well, and FCC Drops the Mars
    Incident," *Broadcasting*, December 15, 1938.
"I wasted . . .": letter from Lewis Long to Welles, October 30, 1938, MICH, box 24.
"taught us . . .": letter to the editor from W. C. Eldridge, "Letters," *Time*,
    November 28, 1938.

DEAR FCC (page 91)

"If some action . . .": letter from James A. Higgins to McNinch, October 31, 1938, NARA,
    box 238.
"I was one . . .": letter from J. V. Yaukey to FCC, November 1, 1938, NARA, box 237.
"It may be well . . .": letter from Thomas Brosnan to the secretary of the interior,
    November 2, 1938, NARA, box 238.
"They performed . . .": letter from John P. Cooney to McNinch, November 2, 1938, NARA,
    box 237.
"I am annoyed . . .": letter from Lynn Montross to Communications Commission,
    November 1, 1938, NARA, box 238.
"We knew it was . . .": letter from Martin Johnson to FCC, November 21, 1938, NARA,
    box 237.
"Having just experienced . . .": letter from Mrs. George J. Newport to United States
    Radio Commission, n.d., NARA, box, 238.
"If a petition . . .": letter from Doris Hurley to McNinch, October 31, 1938, NARA,
    box 238.

"If one has read ...": letter from Lillian Dunston to McNinch, November 3, 1938, NARA, box 237.

"I wouldn't permit ...": letter from Rose A. Flitchman to McNinch, October 31, 1938, NARA, box 238.

"Perhaps you could ...": letter from Mrs. M. L. Purdy to Radio Communication Commission, November 1, 1938, NARA, box 237.

"I have one little ...": letter from T. J. Stansel to McNinch, November 2, 1938, NARA, box 238.

"Dont [sic] you ...": letter from E. P. Clampitt to McNinch, November 1, 1938, NARA, box 237.

"The citizens ...": letter from James W. Smith to Federal Radio Commission, October 31, 1938, NARA, box 238.

"My wife ...": letter from A. C. Patterson to Radio Commission, n.d., NARA, box 238.

"The trouble ...": letter from James H. Jennings to Radio Commission, November 1, 1938, NARA, box 237.

"CBS program ...": telegram from J. M. Smallwood to Chairman Federal Radio and Communication Commission, October 31, 1938, NARA, box 238.

"Those who were ...": letter from A. C. Corcoran, M.D., to McNinch, November 2, 1938, NARA, box 237.

"We need a radio ...": letter from Louis F. Heidenrich to Chairman, FCC, October 31, 1938, NARA, box 238.

"Be assured that ...": letter from Lydel Sims to McNinch, October 31, 1938, NARA, box 237.

CHAPTER THIRTEEN "TOO DARN REALISTIC" (page 94)

"Too Darn ...": letter from Raymond Fischer to WABC, October 30, 1938, MICH, box 24.

"It was only ...": letter to the editor from M. G., "A Few Once-Overs on the Bogymen From Mars," *New York Post*, November 2, 1938.

"mistaken theories ..." and "the ban on ...": Welles, quoted in Johnston and Smith, February 3, 1940, p. 38.

"proper sample ...": Cantril, p. xxix.

"was the only ...": radio listener, quoted in Cantril, p. 100.

CHAPTER FOURTEEN SOFT LANDING (page 99)

"Any man that ...": Anne Wohlk, "AT&T Operators Recall War of the Worlds Broadcast," December 1988, YouTube, AT&T Tech Channel, youtube.com/watch?v=R29BTsoIHpQ &index=10&list=PLWocaE3xRbeqMoxfTAWazPJhUda6Usxle.

"I guess they ...": Houseman, MERC.

"Don't believe everything ...": *Citizen Kane*, screenplay by Herman J. Mankiewicz and Orson Welles, 1941.

"sensational ...": H. G. Wells, "Orson Welles Meets H. G. Wells," October 28, 1940, YouTube, youtube.com/watch?v=nUdghSMTXsU.

"withered and died ...": Houseman, *Front and Center*, p. 107.

"one of the greatest . . .": Paul Stewart, interview with Francois Thomas, March 29, 1982, MICH, box 17.

"He's one of the . . .": Welles, quoted in Rosenbaum, p. 176.

"Without his gifts . . .": Welles, same as above, p. 55.

"What happened to . . .": Koch, quoted in "Spirit of Orson Welles Hovers over 'War of the Worlds' discussion," by Mark Finston, *Sunday Star-Ledger* [NJ], October 30, 1988.

"[Welles] needed . . .": Geraldine Fitzgerald, interview with Frank Beacham, February 24, 1988, MICH, box 14.

"'The War of . . .": Houseman, "The Men from Mars," p. 79.

"an experience . . .": Koch, *The Panic Broadcast*, p. 12.

"I am disappointed . . .": Koch, "War of the Worlds with Orson Wells [*sic*]," NPR Radio Documentary, from October 30, 1988, Part 2, YouTube, youtube.com/watch?v=s7811lx10y4.

"Poisonous black . . .": RADIO.

HOAXES (page 104)

"If the nonexistent . . .": Koch, *The Panic Broadcast*, p. 163.

"How are people . . .": Welles, quoted by Arlene Francis, MERC.

"Awful calamity . . .": *New York Herald*, November 9, 1874.

"Not one word . . .": same as above.

"synchronize . . .": Apple Inc. advertisement, 2014.

"Breaking: Two . . .": Associated Press, Twitter (hacked account), April 23, 2013.

MORE TO EXPLORE (page 110)

"It is impossible . . .": Houseman, "The Men from Mars," p. 79.

AUTHOR'S NOTE (page 118)

"Martians have landed!": New Jersey resident, quoted by Lolly MacKenzie Dey, in "Local residents recall 1938 Martian Panic," by Bill Sanservino, *West Windsor Chronicle, WOW 50th Preview & Guide*, October 20, 1988.

Selected Bibliography

Indicates the primary sources used (letters and telegrams; memoirs; recorded and transcribed interviews; original script, broadcast, and novel)

Bartholomew, Robert E., and Benjamin Radford. *Hoaxes, Myths, and Manias: Why We Need Critical Thinking*. Amherst, NY: Prometheus Books, 2003.

*Beacham, Frank, producer and writer. *Theatre of the Imagination: The Mercury Company Remembers*. Narrated by Leonard Maltin. Sound recording. Santa Monica, CA: Voyager Company, 1988. archive.org/details/OrsonWelles MercuryTheater-1938Recordings.

*Bevilacqua, Joe. *We Take You Now to Grover's Mill: The Making of the "War of the Worlds" Broadcast*. Audiobook. Waterlogg Productions, 2001.

Brady, Frank. *Citizen Welles: A Biography of Orson Welles*. New York: Scribner, 1989.

Brown, Robert J. *Manipulating the Ether: The Power of Broadcast Radio in Thirties America*. Jefferson, NC: McFarland, 1998.

Callow, Simon. *Orson Welles: The Road to Xanadu*. New York: Viking, 1996.

Campbell, W. Joseph. *Getting It Wrong: Ten of the Greatest Misreported Stories in American Journalism*. Berkeley: University of California Press, 2010.

Cantril, Hadley, Hazel Gaudet, and Herta Herzog. *The Invasion from Mars: A Study in the Psychology of Panic*. New Brunswick, NJ: Transaction Publishers, 2005. First published 1940 by Princeton University Press.

Crossley, Robert. "Percival Lowell and the History of Mars." *Massachusetts Review* 41, no. 3 (2000): 297–318.

Dinsman, Melissa. *Modernism at the Microphone: Radio, Propaganda, and Literary Aesthetics During World War II*. London: Bloomsbury Academic, 2015.

*Estrin, Mark W., ed. *Orson Welles: Interviews*. Jackson: University Press of Mississippi, 2002.

*Federal Communications Commission. General Correspondence 1927–1946, Records of the Federal Communications Commission, Record Group 173, file 44–3 (War of the Worlds), National Archives, College Park, MD.

Fedler, Fred. *Media Hoaxes*. Ames: Iowa State University Press, 1989.

Gallop, Alan. *The Martians Are Coming!: The True Story of Orson Welles' 1938 Panic Broadcast*. Stroud, UK: Amberley, 2011.

Gosling, John. *Waging "The War of the Worlds": A History of the 1938 Radio Broadcast and Resulting Panic, Including the Original Script*. Radio Script by Howard Koch. Jefferson, NC: McFarland, 2009.

*Gross, Ben. *I Looked and I Listened: Informal Recollections of Radio and TV*. New York: Random House, 1954.

Herzog, Herta. "Why Did People Believe in the 'Invasion from Mars'?" In *American Broadcasting: A Source Book on the History of Radio and Television*, compiled by Lawrence W. Lichty and Malachi C. Topping. New York: Hastings House, 1975.

Heyer, Paul. "America Under Attack I: A Reassessment of Orson Welles' 1938 'War of the Worlds' Broadcast." *Canadian Journal of Communication* 28, part 2 (2003): 149–165.

_____. *The Medium and the Magician: Orson Welles, the Radio Years, 1934–1952*. Lanham, MD: Rowman and Littlefield, 2005.

*Houseman, John. *Front and Center*. New York: Simon and Schuster, 1979.

*_____. "The Men from Mars." *Harper's Monthly*, December 1948: 74–82.

*_____. *Run-Through: A Memoir*. New York: Simon and Schuster, 1972.

Johnston, Alva, and Fred Smith. "How to Raise a Child: The Education of Orson Welles, Who Didn't Need It." *Saturday Evening Post*, January 20 and 27 and February 3, 1940.

*Koch, Howard. *As Time Goes By: Memoirs of a Writer*. New York: Harcourt Brace Jovanovich, 1979.

*_____. "Invasion from Mars." Radio play, 1938.

*_____. *The Panic Broadcast: Portrait of an Event*. Boston: Little, Brown, 1970.

Lenthall, Bruce. *Radio's America: The Great Depression and the Rise of Modern Mass Culture*. Chicago: University of Chicago Press, 2007.

Lovgen, Stefan. "'War of the Worlds': Behind the 1938 Radio Show Panic." *National Geographic News*, June 17, 2005.

*Lowell, Percival. *Mars*. 2nd ed. Boston: Houghton Mifflin, 1896.

Lowery, Shearon A., and Melvin L. DeFleur. *Milestones in Mass Communication Research: Media Effects*. 3ʳᵈ ed. White Plains, NY: Longman, 1995.

Maloney, Russell. "This Ageless Soul." *The New Yorker*, October 8, 1938: 22–27.

Maltin, Leonard. *The Great American Broadcast: A Celebration of Radio's Golden Age*. New York: Dutton, 1997.

McGilligan, Patrick. *Young Orson: The Years of Luck and Genius on the Path to "Citizen Kane."* New York: Harper, 2015.

Miller, Edward D. *Emergency Broadcasting and 1930s American Radio*. Philadelphia: Temple University Press, 2003.

Naremore, James. *The Magic World of Orson Welles*. Centennial Anniversary Edition. Urbana-Champaign: University of Illinois Press, 2015.

*Orson Welles–Oja Kodar Collection. Special Collections Library, University of Michigan, Ann Arbor.

*Paley, William S. *As It Happened*. Garden City, NY: Doubleday, 1979.

Potter, Lee Ann. "'Jitterbugs' and 'Crack-pots': Letters to the FCC about the 'War of the Worlds' Broadcast." *Prologue: The Journal of the National Archives* 35, no. 3 (2003).

Rabkin, Eric S. *Mars: A Tour of the Human Imagination*. Westport, CT: Praeger, 2005.

Rebecca on *The Campbell Playhouse*, December 9, 1938, radio program.

*Richard Wilson–Orson Welles Papers. Special Collections Library, University of Michigan, Ann Arbor.

*Rosenbaum, Jonathan, ed. *This Is Orson Welles: Orson Welles and Peter Bogdanovich*. New York: HarperCollins, 1992.

Schwartz, A. Brad. *Broadcast Hysteria: Orson Welles's "War of the Worlds" and the Art of Fake News*. New York: Hill and Wang, 2015.

*Smith, David C., ed. *The Correspondence of H. G. Wells*. Vol. 1, 1880–1903. London: Pickering and Chatto, 1998.

Socolow, Michael J. "The Hyped Panic Over 'War of the Worlds.'" *Chronicle of Higher Education*. October 24, 2008.

The War of the Worlds: Mars' Invasion of Earth, Inciting Panic and Inspiring Terror from H. G. Wells to Orson Welles and Beyond. Naperville, IL: Sourcebooks, 2005.

The War of the Worlds on *The Mercury Theatre on the Air*, October 30, 1938, radio program. Based on "Invasion from Mars," script by Howard Koch.

*Wells, H. G. *The War of the Worlds*. New York: Harper and Brothers, 1898.

ADDITIONAL ARTICLES FROM THESE SOURCES:

American Heritage Illustrated
Boston Daily Globe
Broadcasting
Capital Times [Madison, WI]
Charlotte [NC] *News*
Dunkirk [NY] *Evening Observer*
Journal of Communication
Journal of Radio Studies
Los Angeles Daily Mirror
Los Angeles Times
New York Daily News
The New Yorker
New York Journal and American
New York Post
New York Sun
New York Times
New York World-Telegram
Norwalk [CT] *Hour*
Skeptical Inquirer
Smithsonian Magazine
Sunday Star-Ledger [Newark, NJ]
Time magazine
[London] *Times*
Trenton [NJ] *Evening Times*
U.S. 1: Princeton's Business & Entertainment Journal [NJ]
USA Today
Vanity Fair
Wall Street Journal
Washington Post
West Windsor [NJ] *Chronicle*

Index

Page numbers in **boldface** refer to images and/or captions.

A

Associated Press (AP), 62, 107, **107**

B

Bergen, Edgar, 23, **23**, 78
Broun, Heywood, 87

C

Campbell Playhouse, **98**, 99, 102, 108
Cantril, Hadley. *See* Princeton Radio
  Research Project
Chase and Sanborn Hour, The, **23**, 55, 78, 95
Citizen Kane (film), 99, 100, 101
Collins, Ray, **32**, 44
Columbia Broadcasting System (CBS), 20,
  21, 23, 31–33, **32**, 34, **35**, **36–37**, 37–39, 40,
  51, 52, 54–55, 56, 60, 62, 68–70, 72, **73**,
  76, 78, 80, 87–90, **90**, 93, **95**, 95–96, **98**,
  99, 111, **113**
Craven, T. A. M., 84, **84**

D

Danton's Death (play), 32–33, 37, 72
Delmar, Kenny, 38–39, 51, 56, 103, 115

E

Europe in the 1930s, 9–10, **12**, 29, 74, 80,
  84, 87–88, **88**, 104, 115. *See also*
  Nazi Germany

F

Federal Communications Commission
  (FCC), **83**, 83–84, **84**, **88**
    decision on *War of the Worlds*
      broadcast, 89
    letters and telegrams to, **71**, 87–89,
      90, 91–93, 95–96, **113**
Federal Theatre Project, 18–19, **19**, 109
Fitzgerald, Geraldine, 101
Frank, Carl, 62
Froelick, Anne, 24, 31, **31**, 33, 102–103, 109

G

Great Depression, 9, **10**, 14–15, 19, 109
Great War (World War I), 9, 26, 109
Grovers Mill, New Jersey, 30, 54
    broadcast aftermath, 54, 70, **77**,
      102–103, **103**, 108, **108**
    invasion site, 34, 42, 47, 49, 51, 62,
      68, 89

H

Herring, Clyde, 83, **88**, 88–89
Herrmann, Bernard, 23, 32, 36, **37**, 38,
    40–42, 62, 66, 99, 110
Herschel, John, 105
Herschel, William, 27, 105
Herz, William, 103, 109
Hindenburg explosion, **28**, 29, 36, 47, 55,
    103, 109, **109**, 115
Hitler, Adolf, 9–10, **12**, 76, 78, 80, 82, 84, **85**,
    88, 90, 104, 109, **109**
        invasion of Czechoslovakia, 10, 108
        occupation of Austria, 10, 29, 108, 115
hoaxes, 104–107, 117, 119
        Apple iPhone, 106–107
        Associated Press Twitter account,
            107, **107**
        Central Park Zoo Escape, 105–106,
            106
        Great Moon Hoax, 105, **105**
        missing tarantula, 106
Houseman, John, **15**, 72, **73**, 74, 78, 90,
    99–102, **101**, 109, **109**, 110
        actor, 101
        break with Welles, 101
        businessman, 14–15
        childhood, 14
        death, 101, 108
        editor, 101
        theatre producer, 16–20, **19**, **22**, 109
        writer, 15, 17, 21, 23–24, 101.
            See also *Mercury Theatre on the Air*
            (radio show); *War of the Worlds*
            (1938 radio broadcast)
House Un-American Activities
    Committee, 102, 103
Hurricane of 1938, 9, **11**, 69, 90, 92, 108

K

Koch, Howard, **24**, 72, 74, 100–102, 104, 109
        Communist accusation, 102
        death, 102, 109
        lawyer, 24, 102
        writer, 24, 102, 103, 108, 111.
            See also *War of the Worlds* radio
            broadcast: writing of

L

Lindbergh baby kidnapping, 29, 55, 109, 116
Lowell, Percival, 27, 30, 109

M

MacLeish, Archibald, 17, **32**
Marconi, Guglielmo, 29
Mars, 41–42, 44, 49, 54–55, 59, 70, 75, 78,
    82, 89, 92
        canals, 27, 30, 69
        fiction and myth, 27, 29, 79.
            See also *War of the Worlds*
            (serial and novel)
        intelligent life on, 25–27, 29–30,
            104–105, 109
        science of, 27, **27**, 116, **116**
McCarthy, Charlie, 23, **23**, 78, 93
McNinch, Frank, 83, **83**, 87, 89
Mercury Theatre, The (theatre company),
    19–20, 24, **31**, 31–32, 72, **73**, 99, 101,
    109, 116
Mercury Theatre on the Air, The (radio
    show), 20–21, 23–24, **24**, 31, **32**, **36–37**,
    38, 67, 78–80, 95, 97, 99–100, 102–103,
    108, 110–112. See also *War of the Worlds*
    (1938 radio broadcast)

N

Nazi Germany, **12**, 68, 76, 78, **85**, **86**, **88**, 90, 100, 108–109

New Jersey, **28**, 29, 94, 96, 109, **109**, 115
    setting for Martian invasion, 11, 30–31, 34, 41–42, 44, 47, 49, 51, 53–55, 59, 62, 70, 76, 89, 95. *See also* Grovers Mill, New Jersey; Princeton, New Jersey; *War of the Worlds* (1938 radio broadcast): reaction in: New Jersey

newspapers, **16**, 17, 21, 30, 55, 62, 67, 88–89, 94, 96–97, **97**, 104–106, **106**, 117
    War of the Worlds broadcast (1938 radio broadcast)
        articles, **73**, 75–76, **77**, 87, 90, 96
        editorials, 76, 84, 87, 104
        headlines, 74–76, **75**.
        See also *War of the Worlds* (1938 radio broadcast): phone calls to: newspapers

New York City, New York, **10**, 14, 24, 29, 40, 42
    setting for Martian invasion, 13, 30, 34, 55, 59–60, 62, 69, 75, 89
    theatre productions, 15, 18, **19**, 101. *See also War of the Worlds* (1938 radio broadcast): reaction in: New York

Nichols, Ora, 34, **35**, 116

P

Paley, William, 52, 78

Pickering, William, 30

Princeton, New Jersey, 11, 24, 42, 52, 89

Princeton Radio Research Project, 94–96, 108

Princeton University, 30, 70, 87, 94

R

radio in 1930s, 21, 23, **38**, **55**, **95**, **115**, 115–116
    audience size, **8**, 20
    news bulletins, 29
    popularity of, **8**, 20
    programs, 9, 23, **23**, **32**, 34, **35**, 55, 68, **98**, 99. See also *Mercury Theatre on the Air* (radio show)
    sound effects, 21, 23, 34, **35**, **36–37**, 116

Readick, Frank, 36–37, 41, 47, 103, 115

Roosevelt, President Franklin, 11, 38, **38**, 51, 54–55, 87, 109, 115

S

Schiaparelli, Giovanni, 27, 30

Seymour, Dan, 40, 60

Stewart, Paul, 24, 31, 33–34, 36, 38–39

T

Taylor, Davidson, 38, 51, 56

telephone operators, 52–53, **53**, 99, 112

Thompson, Dorothy, 84, **85**

W

War of the Worlds (1938 radio broadcast), 11, 13, 29, 78–79, 97, 100, **103**, 103–104, 108, 110–112, 118–119
    audience size, 52, 94–95, **95**
    lawsuits, 89–90
    letters and telegrams about, 68–70, **69**, 76, 88. *See also* Federal Communications Commission: letters and telegrams to; Welles, Orson: letters and telegrams to
    music, **37**, 37–39, 40–42, 44, 47, 62
    on-air performance, 40–42, 44, 47, 49, 51, 56, 59–60, 62, 66, 89
    phone calls to
        newspapers, 53, 62, 76, 89
        police, 53, 70, **71**, 75–76, 89
        radio stations, 51–53, 72, 76–77, 96

telephone operators, 52–53, 112

physical responses, 55, 68–69,
    75–76, 78

reaction in
    colleges, 54, 68
    Columbia Broadcasting System
        (CBS) headquarters, 51–52, 56,
        72, 78, 87, 89, 99
    Europe, 76, 87
    Midwest, 55, 68, 72, 76, 80–82,
        88–93
    New England, 55, 68–69, 76, 82,
        88, 91–92
    New Jersey, 9, 52, 54, 67, 70–71,
        71, 75, 80, 82, 87–88, **90**, 92
    New York, 52, 54, 62, 67–70, 72,
        75, 75–76, 81–82, 88–89,
        91–92, 96
    Pennsylvania, 68
    South, 55, 69–70, 80–81, 87,
        89–90, 92–93
    West, 52, 55, 68, 70, 76, 80–82,
        91–93
    rehearsal, 31–32, 34, 36–39
    sound effects, 34, 37, **37**, 39
    writing of, 29–34, 66, 102, 118

War of the Worlds (radio broadcasts after
    1938), 96–97, **97**

War of the Worlds (serial and novel),
    25–27, 29–32, 34, 40–41, 44, 49, 52, 56,
    60, 62, 66, 78, 89, 97, 100, 117–118
    images from, **front and back
        covers**, **front and back jacket
        flaps**, **1–3**, **26**,**40**, **43**, **45–50**, **56–61**,
        63–65, **74**, **109**, **111**, **141**, **144**

Welles, Orson, 72, **73**, 90, 94, 104, **114**, 115
    actor
        film, 99
        radio, 20, **20**, 31, **32**, **98**, 99, 103,
            110, 116
        theatre, 17–19, **20**, 109
    break with Houseman, 101

childhood, **16**, 17–18, 109, **109**

death, 100, 108

director, 17–21, **19**, **22**, 23–24,
    32–33, **36–37**, 37–39, 109

education, 17–18

letters and telegrams to, 80–83,
    95–96

meeting H. G. Wells, 99–100,
    100, 108, **108**, 112

press conference, October 31, 1938,
    78–79, **79**, 111

writer, 21, 23–24, 102.
See also *Mercury Theatre on the
    Air* (radio show); *War of the
    Worlds* (1938 radio broadcast)

Wells, H. G., 25, **25**, 27, 29, 78, 108, **108**
    death, 100, 108
    meeting Orson Welles, 100, **100**,
        108, **108**, 112
    published works, 25. See also *War
        of the Worlds* (serial and novel)

Work Progress Administration, 19

World War II, **86**, **100**, 108, 116

Picture Credits

Associated Press Images: 100, 108 (middle).

Alvim Corrêa, illustrator, in H. G. Wells, *La Guerre Des Mondes* (*The War of the Worlds*), Jette-Bruxelles (Belgium): L. Vandamme, 1906: front and back covers, front jacket flap, back jacket flap, 1–3, 26 (left), 40, 43, 45, 46, 48, 49, 50, 56, 57, 58, 59, 61, 63, 74, 111, 141, 144.

Flickr: Creative Commons Attribution 2.0: 28, 109 (bottom left).

Warwick Goble, illustrator, in H. G. Wells, *The War of the Worlds*, New York: Harper & Brothers, 1898: 47, 60, 64–65, 109 (middle left).

Historical Findings: 31, 73.

Reprinted by permission of **Peter Koch**: 24.

Library of Congress, Prints & Photographs Division, LC-USZ62-54357: 8; LC-USZ62-12667: 12; LC-DIG-ppmsca-18743: 88 (top); LC-USZ62-109377: 109 (bottom right); Carl Van Vechten Collection, LC-USZ62-119765: 20; Farm Security Administration/Office of War Information Photograph Collection: LC-USF34-040293-D: 11; LC-USW3-016733-C: 55; LC-USF34-035128-D: 69; LC-USW33-000890-ZC: 86; LC-USF34-037961-D: 95; LC-USF3301-011602-M2: 115; George Grantham Bain Collection: LC-B2-3798-1: 25, 108 (top); Harris & Ewing Collection: LC-H21-C-774-A: 38; LC-H22-D-2048: 53; LC-H22-D5483: 83; LC-H22-D-2221: 84; LC-H22-D-6427: 85; LC-H25-110206-C: 88 (bottom); Landauer Collection of Aeronautical Prints and Drawings: LC-USZ62-25422: 105; *New York World-Telegram and the Sun* Newspaper Photograph Collection: LC-USZ62-115090: 10; LC-USZ62-126188: 23; LC-USZ62-112306: 98; Work Projects Administration Poster Collection, LC-USZC2-5607: 19.

Los Angeles **[CA]** *Daily Mirror*, February 14, 1949: 97.

Mary Evans Picture Library: 77, 79.

National Aeronautics and Space Administration (NASA): Neil Armstrong, photographer: 26 (right); JPL-Caltech: 27, 116.

National Archives and Records Administration: 71, 90, 113 (top and bottom).

New York Herald, November 9, 1874: 106.

New York Public Library for the Performing Arts, Billy Rose Theatre Division, Astor, Lenox and Tilden Foundations: 15, 22, 32, 35, 36–37, 109 (top).

New York Telegram, October 31, 1938: 75 (bottom).

Ogdensburg **[NY]** *Journal*, October 31, 1938: 75 (top).

Twitter, April 23, 2013: 107.

Wikimedia Commons: 16, 109 (middle right), 114; by Alan Light, Creative Commons Attribution 2.0 Generic: 101; by ZeWrestler: 103, 108 (bottom).

The final illustration of the 1906 edition of *The War of the Worlds* shows its creators, illustrator Alvim Corrêa (left) and H. G. Wells.

GAIL JARROW is the author of numerous nonfiction books, including *Bubonic Panic*, *Fatal Fever*, and *Red Madness*, a trilogy on deadly diseases. The most valuable lesson she has learned from studying science and history is to question assertions, analyze evidence, and dig deeper for the truth. Gail's books have received many distinctions, including a YALSA Award Nomination for Excellence in Nonfiction, an NCSS Notable Social Studies Trade Book, the Jefferson Cup Award, and an NSTA Best STEM Book. She lives in Ithaca, New York. Visit her at gailjarrow.com.

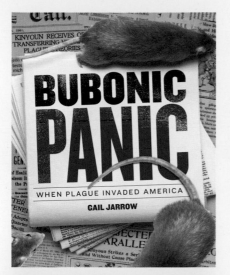

BUBONIC PANIC:
WHEN PLAGUE INVADED AMERICA

★ *Publishers Weekly*, starred review
★ *School Library Journal*, starred review
★ *Kirkus Reviews*, starred review
Kirkus Reviews Best Teen Books of the Year
School Library Journal Best Books of the Year
NSTA Outstanding Science Trade Books for Children
NCSS Notable Social Studies Trade Books for Children

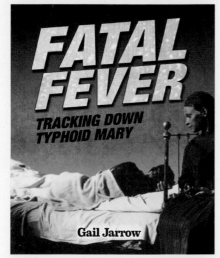

FATAL FEVER:
TRACKING DOWN TYPHOID MARY

★ *Publishers Weekly*, starred review
★ *School Library Journal*, starred review
★ *Kirkus Reviews*, starred review
★ *Booklist*, starred review
The Bulletin of the Center for Children's Books, Blue Ribbon List
VOYA Nonfiction Honor List
International Literacy Association, Best Science Books of the Year

RED MADNESS:
HOW A MEDICAL MYSTERY
CHANGED WHAT WE EAT

★ *School Library Journal*, starred review
★ *Kirkus Reviews*, starred review
School Library Journal Best Books of the Year
NSTA Best STEM Books
Virginia Library Association Jefferson Cup Award